Isles of Gold

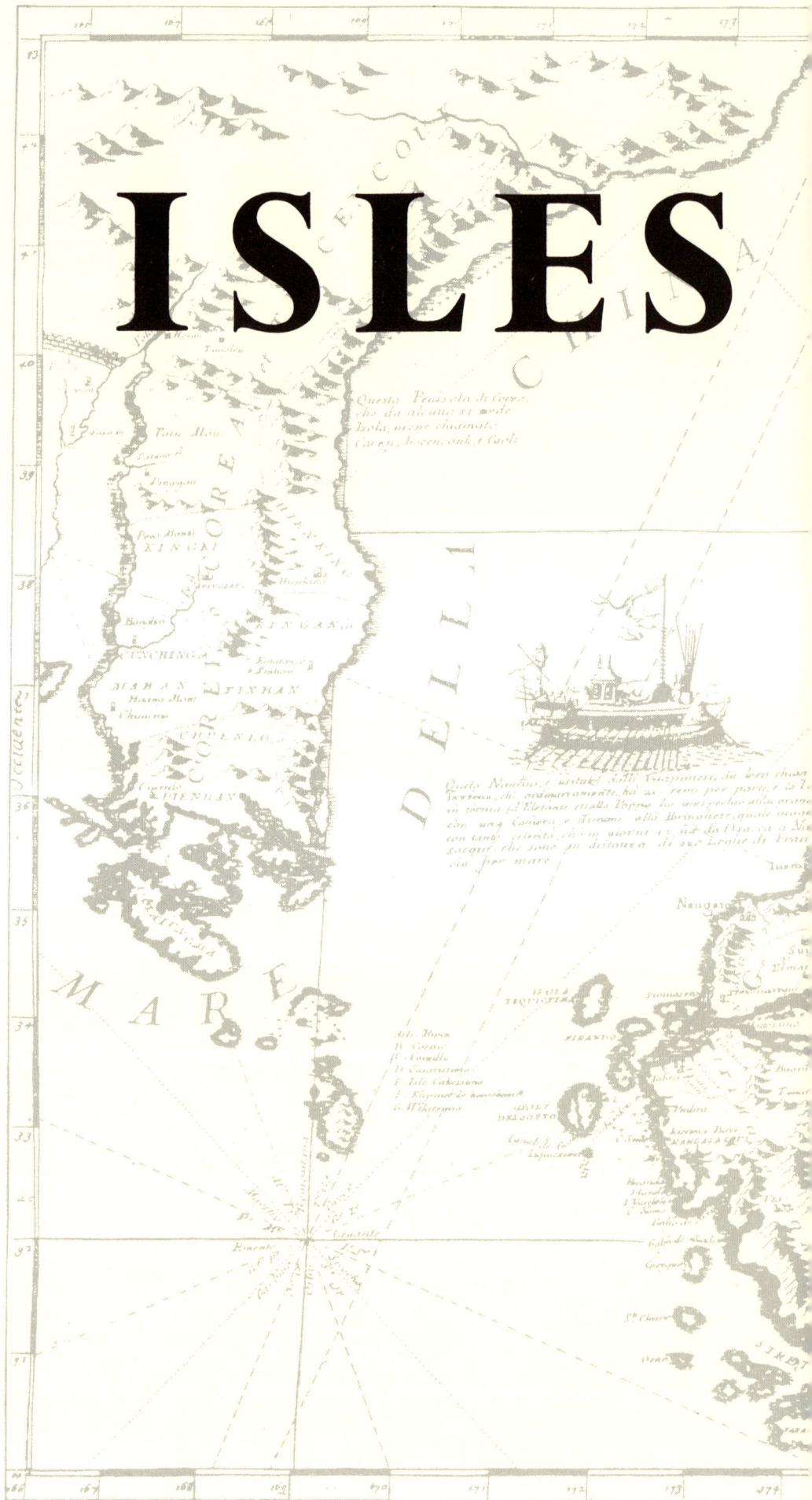

ISLES

Questa Penisola di Corea,
che da alcuni si mede
Isola, viene chiamata:
Caven, Iocenchuk, e Cacli

Questa Nauilio, è usitato dalli Giapponesi, da loro chiamato
Turrena, che ordinariamente ha... remi per parte, e la...
in vecina d'Elefante alla Poppa, da una pecchio alla arena...
con una Canoa, e Timone alla Bermudez quale naviga...
con tanta celerità, ca in giorni 15 va da Chinca a Noci...
sacque, che sono in distanza di 210 Leone di Varia...
... per mare

HUGH CORTAZZI

OF GOLD
Antique Maps of Japan

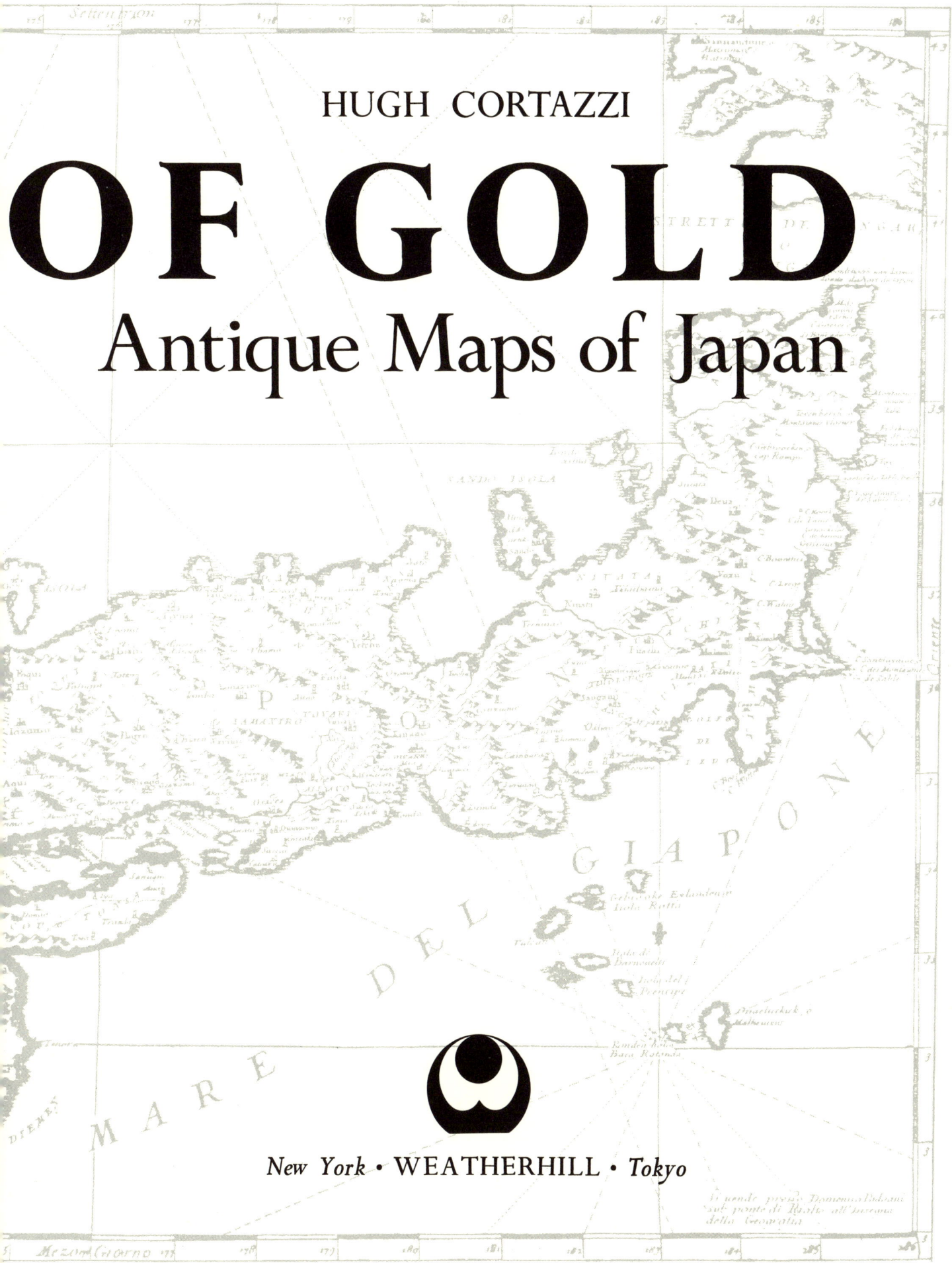

New York • WEATHERHILL • *Tokyo*

ISLES OF GOLD: Antique Maps of Japan was published
with the assistance of grants from
ScanDutch I/S (Partnership) of Copenhagen
and
the Japan Foundation, Tokyo

First edition, 1983

Published by John Weatherhill, Inc., of New York and Tokyo, with editorial offices at 7–6–13
Roppongi, Minato-ku, Tokyo 106, Japan. Copyright © 1983 by Hugh Cortazzi; all rights reserved.
Printed and first published in Japan.

Library of Congress Cataloging in Publication Data: Cortazzi, Hugh. / Isles of gold. / 1. Japan—
Maps. 2. Japan—Maps, Pictorial. 3. Japan—Maps—Facsimiles. 4. Japan—Maps, Pictorial—Facsimiles. 5. Maps, Early—Facsimiles. I. Title. / GA1241.C67 1983 912'. 52 / 83–3525 / ISBN
0–8348–0184–1

To Elizabeth

Contents

Plates

Preface

My wife and I became interested quite by chance in old maps of Japan. One day in the mid-1960s, my wife told me that she had seen an interesting old map of Japan in the window of a bookshop in Kanda, the main bookselling area of Tokyo. I went to have a look at it and found that it was a Kaempfer map of about 1727. Later, when we were on leave in Britain, we amused ourselves by combing the shops which specialized in old maps for any maps they had of Japan. We became more and more fascinated by these maps. Many of them, with their cartouches and other decorations such as depictions of sailing ships or dolphins, struck us as works of art in their own right, especially if they had been hand-colored in an earlier age (European maps were originally printed in black and white). They also seemed to me to be of great historical interest, as they revealed the progress not only of Western knowledge of Japan but also of European discoveries in the Far East.

We bought maps from famous London map sellers, such as Robert Douwma, Map House in Beauchamp Place, and Baynton Williams in Lowndes Street. But we also found the odd map in country shops, and when we were in the United States in the early 1970s, we discovered one or two good examples in New York. One of the joys of collecting is, of course, the occasional find in out-of-the-way places, but persistence and patience are also needed—it took us over fifteen years, for example, to find one small Dutch map of Japan which we particularly wanted, the 1707 map of Japan by Pieter van der Aa. Inevitably, collecting can be an expensive hobby. There are also difficulties in identification and dating. Most of the old European printed maps of Japan come from atlases which have been broken up. Many atlases were reprinted frequently, and it requires an expert knowledge of the different editions, of watermarks, and of paper to identify accurately the date of a particular map. Similar expertise is required to distinguish between early and later coloring. But the collector can usually rely on the advice of the reputable map sellers, though even they frequently can do no more than give an approximate date. As in all collecting, it is best to choose what interests and attracts rather than simply go for the rarity. We were fortunate that when we began our collection, European maps of Japan had not become so popular with Japanese collectors as they are now, and I fear that our days of collecting old Japanese maps are largely over.

Those early European maps of Japan inevitably aroused our curiosity about Japanese maps of Japan and, in particular, the influence of Japanese mapmakers on their European counterparts and vice versa. An exhibition of Chinese and Japanese maps at the British Museum in 1974 acted as a spur to further study. I realized that Japanese maps, too, were works of art as well as fascinating historical artifacts.

Unfortunately, really old Japanese printed maps of Japan are generally even more expensive than European maps of comparable date. However, it is still possible to find interesting and attractive old Japanese maps in, for instance, some of the old book and print shops in Kanda. These are mainly nineteenth-century or late-Edo– period maps, occasionally of Japan as a whole or of the world as seen through Japanese eyes at the time. Maps of Edo, Kyoto, and other Japanese cities can be found, Edo maps being the most generally available. A number of modern reprints of old Japanese and European maps of Japan have been produced in recent years.

One problem with old Japanese maps produced in Japan is their size. Many are large in format, and the constant folding and unfolding resulting from their size inevitably caused splits and tears. Japanese maps were generally designed to be studied while sitting on the floor and are frequently omnidirectional. Moreover, the paste in the paper used in Japan seems to have been particularly attractive to worms, and many Japanese maps have, as a consequence, wormholes. While European maps were usually printed from copper plates, Japanese maps, especially early ones, were printed from wood blocks.

It was only after I came to Japan as British Ambassador in the autumn of 1980 that

I really began a serious study of the subject. In a rash moment I offered to give a lecture to the Asiatic Society of Japan about old maps of Japan, and then I really had to get down to the necessary research.

Earlier, I had acquired a copy of Tony Campbell's monograph published by the Map Collectors' Circle (Fourth volume, No. 36) entitled *Japan: European Printed Maps to 1800*. This is an invaluable little work for the collector, but it does not claim to be much more than an annotated list. I soon found that in addition to Graf Teleki's monumental work in German, *Atlas zur Geschichte der Kartographie der Japanischen Inseln*, published in Budapest in 1909, there were many other works and articles in English and French as well as, of course, numerous books in Japanese by eminent Japanese scholars on the subject. There are also a number of interesting articles in learned publications, especially *Imago Mundi*. But I could not find any single, generally accessible work in English which both summarized the development of old maps of Japan, European and Japanese, and at the same time provided a reasonably clear account of the interrelationship of the two traditions. This is what I have attempted to do in this volume, which is an expansion of the lecture that I gave to the Asiatic Society of Japan in January, 1982. The 1982 *Transactions of the Asiatic Society of Japan* contains the text of the article on which my lecture was based. This included detailed references. I have appended a short bibliography to this volume for any reader who wishes to delve more deeply.

I should add that one fascination about the study of old maps is that it leads on to other studies, especially in the fields of history and geography, but also in the art and culture of the country in question. The more one studies any subject, but especially, perhaps, a subject that one at first thinks mistakenly has been relatively neglected, the more one realizes the depths of one's own ignorance. I do not pretend that this work is comprehensive. Indeed, in the short space of a volume of this size this would not be possible. Collectors will inevitably find old European and Japanese maps of Japan which are not mentioned here, and I will inevitably have left out a reference to someone's favorite map. But I hope that this summary of the subject up to the middle of the nineteenth century, when the Japanese coastline and interior had been pretty accurately surveyed, will be of interest to the general reader. Also, in the interest of the general reader, I have tried to follow the most commonly used orthography of the names of European cartographers, though variations abound. For variant names and spellings the reader is referred to the list of cartographers appended to Raymond Lister's *Old Maps and Globes* (Revised edition, London, 1979) as well as the aforementioned work by Tony Campbell.

I should like to express my particular thanks to Weatherhill for all their help and advice in the production of this book—in particular, I should like to thank Jeff Hunter for his careful editing, although I must accept responsibility for any inaccuracies which may have inadvertently crept into the text. I am also grateful to Miriam Yamaguchi for her encouragement.

I must record my especial thanks to ScanDutch I/S (Partnership) of Copenhagen and the Japan Foundation for their sponsorship of this work.

I owe a debt of gratitude to many others for their generous help and advice. It would be invidious to try to list these in any order suggesting the measure of their help. Instead, I have chosen to list them alphabetically. The following institutions have all been of great assistance: the Archivio di Stato in Florence; British Library, especially Helen Wallis of the Map Room, Kenneth Gardner of the Department of Oriental Manuscripts and Printed Books, and Anthony Farrington of the India Office Library and Records; Henry E. Huntington Library, San Marino, California; Hōryū-ji, Nara; Jōtoku-ji, Fukui; Kanazawa Bunko, Yokohama; Kobe City Museum; Maeda Ikutokukai, Tokyo; Maspro Denkow Art Gallery, Aichi; Namban Bunkakan, Osaka; National Diet Library, Tokyo; National Museum of Japanese History, Chiba; Ninna-ji, Kyoto; Okayama University; Shōsō-in, Nara; Tenri Central Library, Nara; Tōdai-ji, Nara; and Tōshōdai-ji, Nara. These individuals also deserve special mention for their assistance: Adriana Boscaro of the Institute of Japanese Studies in Venice; Tony Campbell of Douwma Map Sellers for much useful advice; Dr. Michael Cooper, Sophia University, Tokyo, for indefatigable and invaluable help and advice; and Mr. J.K. Matsumura of the British Embassy, for great patience and an immense amount of help in getting specialist material and finding out answers to innumerable questions. I should also like to thank my secretaries, Ann Wiles, Julie Adam, and Pam Simpson for their help in preparing the text by typing and retyping my manuscripts.

Essay: Isles of Gold

Early Maps of Japan

Early Japanese Maps

Maps were first needed in Japan, as in other countries, to confirm landholdings and their locations. But in the period before Chinese and Buddhist influence began to be strongly felt in Japan in the sixth and seventh centuries, the system of land tenure under the clans who then ruled Japan appears to have been primitive. Indeed, the concept of property in land was not understood in what was almost exclusively an agricultural economy; land without labor for its cultivation does not represent wealth. However, as Chinese influence grew and Chinese writing was adopted for record keeping in the fifth and sixth centuries, the imperial government tried to foster the idea that the provincial rulers held their territory as delegates of the emperor. This was based on the Chinese doctrine that "under the wide heavens there is no place which is not the king's land." In the latter part of the seventh century, the system of allotting land according to the number of members of each household (the *ku-bun-den*, or literally, "mouth-share-field" system) was officially adopted. In fact, the system was probably never much more than an ideal, and local chieftains and temples soon began to stake out claims to major landholdings and became officially recognized owners of property. Thus, the first maps in Japan seem to have been diagrams of landholdings or estates. There are some maps of this type in the Shōsō-in, the old treasure house of Nara, which contains the personal belongings of Emperor Shōmu that were dedicated in 756 to the Buddha of the Tōdai-ji in Nara by his widow. They have remained largely intact to this day. One of the Shōsō-in maps of Minuma village in Ōmi Province (now Shiga Prefecture) is dated 751.

The Tōdai-ji in Nara also possessed several maps of newly developed rice fields from roughly the same period (Pl. 1). These maps have survived because they were drawn on cloth. They appear to have been based on reasonably accurate measurements. Some of these estate maps included topographical particulars and points of the compass. Although it cannot be confirmed that primitive compasses reached Japan from China until the eleventh century, the way in which early Japanese temples were built suggests some knowledge of magnetic compasses from the Nara period.

Maps were, however, referred to even earlier, even if none have survived. During the Taika Reforms (ca. 645), when Japan was adopting Chinese customs and laws, an order, recorded in one of Japan's earliest histories, the *Nihongi*, was issued: "The boundaries of the provinces should be examined and a description or map prepared which should be brought here and produced for our [imperial] inspection." Thereafter, in both the Nara (710–93) and Heian (794–1185) periods, orders were issued that maps of the provinces and their subdivisions should be made. We do not know how far these instructions were obeyed, as no such maps have survived. Even though many of these orders were probably ignored by the local chieftains, whose fiefs never came under the same control as did the provinces in China during the Tang dynasty (618–907), some maps must surely have been drawn. In 682 a map of Tanegashima off the southern coast of Kyushu and another of Shinano Province (now Nagano Prefecture) are recorded as having been presented at court.

The father and founder of Japanese mapmaking, according to Japanese tradition, was Gyōgi Bosatsu, a Buddhist priest of Korean descent who lived from about 688 to 749. Gyōgi is said to have traveled throughout Japan, not only spreading the message of Buddhism but also teaching the arts of constructing roads, bridges, canals, and dams. Indeed, he seems to have been one of Japan's first civil engineers. He apparently played a prominent part at the court when Nara was the capital during the reign of Emperor Shōmu (724–48). It is therefore probable that the order which was issued in 738 about the drawing of provincial maps may have been inspired by him. There is, however, no actual proof that Gyōgi ever produced any maps himself.

4

At any rate, none have survived from this period. Nevertheless, the term "Gyōgi-type maps" came to be used in Japan for diagrams or primitive drawings which showed the interrelationship of the provinces with the capital as well as the seven regions and five special provinces nearest the capital. Professor Charles Boxer said of Gyōgi-type maps that they "normally list the names of the provinces, main highways and provincial subdivisions in marginal explanatory notes after the style of a concise gazetteer." But their most notable feature was the way in which they depicted the provinces in balloon shapes (round or oval) clustered around Kyoto, the capital. The main purpose of Gyōgi-type maps seems to have been to show the relationship of the provinces with one another and with the capital.

The oldest surviving original of a Gyōgi-type map (Pl. 2), dated 1305, is held by the Ninna-ji in Kyoto. This is a rough and primitive map with few place names and with the western half, including Kyushu and part of western Honshu, missing. Some additions appear to have been made by a later hand. A noteworthy feature of this and other early maps produced in Japan is that south is at the top of the map and, as a consequence, China and Korea appear on the right. The two northern provinces of Honshu, Mutsu and Dewa, point outward, whereas in other Gyōgi-type maps they are usually shown in rounded form.

An early Gyōgi-type map was included in the tenth volume of the *Nichūreki*. The *Nichūreki* (Two Guides) was, as its title suggests, a compilation of two earlier guide-books, or gazetteers, the *Shōchūreki* (Handy Guide) and the *Kaichūreki* (Pocket Guide). The "map" in the *Nichūreki*, actually little more than a string of names of provinces in simple, diagrammatic form, first apeared in the *Kaichūreki*. Though the *Nichūreki* was first compiled in 1128, the *Nichūreki* map in Plate 3 dates from the fourteenth century and is part of a manuscript in the possession of the Maeda Ikuto-kukai Foundation, Tokyo.

Another Gyōgi-type map (Pl. 4) is in the famous Kanazawa Bunko library. It, too, is of about 1305 and has south at the top, but it is incomplete: this time the eastern half is missing. An interesting and unusual feature of this map is that it is framed by a dragon. Significantly, the map mentions territories outside Japan, including Mōkokoku (the country of the Mongols). It also depicts the islands of Shikano and Takeshima, where fierce fighting occurred during the Mongol attacks on Japan in 1274 and 1281.

One other early Japanese map must be mentioned. This is a sixteenth-century manuscript copy (ca. 1557, Pl. 5) of an earlier map and has been preserved by the Tōshōdai-ji in Nara, although the map originally came from another Nara temple and came into the hands of the Tōshōdai-ji only around the Meiji Restoration. It is known as the *Nansembushū Dainihonkoku Shōtōzu*, which may be translated as the "Authorized Map of Great Japan and the World." Nansembushū is a Buddhist word derived from the Sanskrit, Jambudvīpa, or "the southern continent." This term was used to describe India, and by extension, the entire world, in ancient Indian cosmology. The map has Kyushu at the top and Tōhoku at the bottom and is surrounded by a commentary; it places Mount Fuji in Suruga Province (the modern Shizuoka Prefecture), and Aizu to the south of the two northerly provinces of Mutsu and Dewa. Akita castle is shown in Dewa. The commentary refers to 615 *gun*, or districts. The shape of Japan is still very impressionistic and inaccurate, and Kyushu and Shikoku are compressed while the size of the Inland Sea is exaggerated.

An interesting feature of these early Gyōgi-type maps was the inclusion of two fabulous countries—Rasetsukoku to the south and Gandō (or Kari no Michi) to the north. Rasetsukoku is the country of the Rasetsu (Sanskrit, *rākṣasa* or *rakshasa*), who were female demons. Ten Rakshasas are named in the Lotus Sutra, perhaps the most important of all the sutras in the Buddhist canon as far as Japanese Buddhists are concerned. In the sutra, they undertook to "protect those who read and recite, receive and keep the Law-Flower sutra," and were duly praised by the Buddha for this pious promise. The Rakshasa in Japanese myths and stories were, however, unregenerate female demons reputed to eat shipwrecked wanderers who were unfortunate enough to come their way. This fable was first recorded in the fifth book of the *Konjaku Monogatari* (Tales of Times Now Past), a collection of stories and fables produced in the late Heian period (about 1050), including Buddhist legends, ghost stories, and battle accounts. In the version of the tale appearing in the *Konjaku*

6

Monogatari, sailors shipwrecked on an uncharted island are warmly welcomed by its inhabitants—ravishingly beautiful women. The sailor swed their hostesses, only to find that they are, in reality, demons who devour their "husbands" and take new ones each time a ship is wrecked near their shores. The continued appearance of this mythological island on Gyōgi-type maps has been ascribed to the influence of the Buddhist monks who were the scholars and copyists of the time and who wished to warn their male followers against the temptations of the opposite sex. Later, in the Tokugawa period (1600–1868), Rasetsukoku was sometimes replaced by Nyōgoga-shima, meaning simply "the island of women." In the novel *Kōshoku Ichidai Otoko* (The Man Who Loved Love), published in 1682 by Ihara Saikaku, the hero, after twenty-seven years of dissipation, builds a ship with a white sail made from silken female undergarments, loads on it aphrodisiacs and *shunga* (erotic pictures), and sets out for the island of Nyōgo. He tells his companions that he will there introduce them to a different type of female, "the aggressive sort who will come to seize you and sweep you off your feet." For whatever reason, the travelers never return. Rasetsukoku was placed in the neighborhood of Hachijōjima on maps by Ishikawa Ryūsen (see Pl.41). Eventually it was realized that there was only one island there, and Rasetsukoku was assimilated into Hachijōjima.

The name of the second mythical land, Gandō, or Kari no Michi, can be translated as "the route of the wild geese," suggesting a knowledge of bird migration. In the Kanazawa Bunko map, a note records that while there was a castle there, there were no inhabitants on the island. Perhaps Ezo or Yezo (later Hokkaido) was intended. A striking feature of all the Gyōgi-type maps was, in fact, the absence of any direct mention of Ezo, which came to be called Hokkaido only after the Meiji Restoration of 1868. This reflected the Japanese lack of any real interest in the island and the other territories to the north until the seventeenth and eighteenth centuries, when the potential Russian threat began to be felt. Even the north of Honshu was, as we have seen, not well known and was generally very inaccurately depicted. Tōhoku (the Northeast), as this region was called, was in these early days still occupied in part at least by the "Barbarians," or "Ebisu," who were the ancestors of the Ainu of Hokkaido. Imperial rule did not extend effectively much beyond Kantō, the area around modern Tokyo, until the early Heian period, and even then the imperial forces were somewhat in the nature of an occupying army. The main headquarters of the imperial government in Tōhoku in the eleventh and twelfth centuries was Hiraizumi (north of Sendai and now part of Iwate Prefecture). The more northerly parts were little known, and it is therefore hardly surprising that the general shape of the region was only guessed at. As a result, Tōhoku on early Japanese maps was compressed and often shown in an almost horizontal east-west position or even turning southward.

Almost certainly, the first Japanese printed map was of the Gyōgi type. This was probably the map in the *Shūgaishō* (Pl.6), first printed during the Keichō era (1596–1615). The *Shūgaishō* (Collection of Oddments) was a simple gazetteer similar to the *Nichūreki* (see p. 5). It was first produced in 1291, and a number of different versions followed, including an expanded version in 1360. Copies dating from before the first printing lack the map, which is on a small scale (27.5 x 17.5 centimeters), covering two pages of the book. South was still at the top. The provinces were named and the main areas were marked.

A number of Gyōgi-type maps found their way to China and Korea, and Gyōgi-type depictions of Japan appeared on printed Chinese and Korean maps before they were printed in Japan. One example was the *Hai Tong Che Kukki* (Record of the Countries in the Eastern Sea), which was the first individual map of Japan to appear in Korea. It was produced from a woodblock print in 1471 and was drawn by one Shin Suk Ju, a Korean who had been sent on a mission to Japan. Another example was the *Erben Kaolüe* (Summary of Japan), which was produced in China from a woodblock in 1523. The area around modern Tokyo was shown as if it formed an island, and Tōhoku was depicted as turning southward. This is interesting in view of the way some European cartographers in the late sixteenth century also showed Tōhoku pointing south. Indeed, it is probable that some of these maps were studied by Europeans in Macao and may have helped European cartographers in their early efforts to depict Japan on their maps (see also p.11).

Gyōgi-type maps continued to appear even in the Tokugawa, or Edo, period. Maps were frequently used during this period to decorate items of everyday use. Gyōgi-type maps were almost invariably used for this purpose, even in the first half of the nineteenth century, when the cartography of the Japanese islands had made significant progress. One of the earliest examples was a map on a fan which belonged to Toyotomi Hideyoshi (1536–98), one of the great military rulers of Japan, who succeeded the previous military ruler Oda Nobunga (1534–82) and attempted the conquest of Korea. Another was the map on the back of a metal mirror presented by the military leader Katō Kiyomasa (1562–1611) to the Kitano Shrine in Kyoto. This was made by Kise Jōami, a famous metalworker of the period, between 1598 and 1611. In the private collection of Mr. Y. Kitamura in his Namban (Southern Barbarian) Bunkakan in Osaka there are a number of other examples, including maps on *tsuba* (sword guards, Pl.7), *inrō* (medicine cases, Pl.8), and even netsuke (Pl.9). Gyōgi-type maps were also frequently used to decorate porcelain, especially Imari ware (Pl. 10) but also Kutani and Genna wares.

Until the Portuguese arrived in the sixteenth century, Japanese knowledge of the outside world was limited to what they had learned through Korea and China. Beyond these countries, they were really only conscious of the existence of India, whence Buddhism had come to Japan via China and Korea. The account of the pilgrimage to India of Xuanzhuang, a Chinese priest, in the seventh century, inspired the Japanese to draw maps including the imaginary continent of Jambudvipa. In Indian cosmology, this represented the whole of the inhabited world. A fourteenth-century copy of one such map is preserved in the Hōryū-ji near Nara. This is entitled *Gotenjikuzu* (Map of the Five Regions of India, Pl.11). Tenjiku, or India, is placed in the center, with large, snow-covered mountains and the sources of the world's four great rivers to the north. China appears to the east, and Japan is in the sea to the northeast. Ceylon is shown in the southeast.

In the early days when there were no real maps, the Gyōgi-type diagrams represented real cartographic progress, and it would be unreasonable to expect anything much better in the fourteenth century, when European mapmaking was also very primitive and inaccurate. But although the Gyōgi-type maps gradually improved, they never contained much in the way of geographical information, and the shape of the Japanese islands became stereotyped, so that even when mapmakers knew better they tended to follow the old patterns. This kind of stereotyping was a common feature of many other aspects of Japanese culture from the eleventh to the nineteenth century, including poetry, which remained frozen in the *waka* or *tanka* form of thirty-one syllables; theatre arts, which developed a stereotyped shorthand in the form of conventional costuming, makeup, and dance movement; and even the martial arts, which were reduced to a standard language of gesture known as *kata*. This conservative tendency toward standardization was equally strong in Japanese mapmaking. Alessandro Valignano, the late-sixteenth–century Jesuit Visitor, commented on Japanese cartography in the following terms: "From olden times the Japanese have had geographical maps of all these islands, but as they had no knowledge of cosmography and knew nothing about degrees and the elevation of the pole, they had no reliable and good drawings. They also did not know accurately the position and latitude of the islands."

Though Japanese maps in these early days provided a vague idea of the general shape of Japan and the interrelationship of the provinces, cartography, hindered by conventions, remained primitive.

Early European Maps

While Japanese cartography was primitive in medieval times, Western cartographers, at least up to the arrival of the first Europeans in Japan in the sixteenth century, were either totally ignorant of the country or, at best, had only the haziest idea of where Japan was or what its shape was. The founder of European geography, Ptolemy, who worked and lived in Alexandria in the second century A.D., knew nothing of Japan. Basing himself on Greek and Latin scholarship, he developed relatively advanced astronomical methods, but he had little knowledge of the world beyond the Mediterranean area, although he amassed a great deal of geographical information. None of Ptolemy's original maps, said to have numbered twenty-six, have survived, but the Ptolemaic tradition was kept alive through the Middle Ages, and his influence lasted up to the sixteenth century. The Swiss cartographer Sebastian Münster (1489–1552) produced an edition of Ptolemy's atlas in 1540 in which he included a map of the New World showing Japan (Pl. 12), under the name "Zipangri," in a roughly oblong shape extending from north to south off the west coast of America. This, as is explained below, was by no means the first depiction of Japan on a European map.

Japan was, however, unknown to the medieval geographers. The beautiful world map in Hereford Cathedral in England, drawn about 1300 by Richard de Bello, includes China under the name "Seres" (marked as famous for silk) but makes no mention of Japan. Asia, interestingly, forms the upper half of the map, meaning east was at the top. However, some other (pre-Münster) editions of Ptolemy's *Geographia* refer to 7,548 islands off the coast of China. These were also mentioned in the *Catalan Atlas* of 1375 by the Majorcan Jew Abraham Cresques, cartographer to the king of Aragon. The atlas was presented to King Charles V of France in 1381 and is preserved in the Bibliothèque Nationale in Paris.

Persian geographical writings in the ninth century referred to an island east of China and Korea called "Wakwak." This may have been a corruption of "Wa-Kuo" (or Wa-Kwok), an old Sino-Korean name for Japan, the country of the Wa, or people of short stature. The character then used for *wa*, meaning dwarf, was later replaced by a homophonous character meaning peace, but both can also be read in Japanese as "Yamato," which is the name the Japanese used in ancient and even in more modern times to refer to their land. The earliest Chinese reference to the country of the Wa is thought to have been in 264 B.C., but it is not confirmed that Wa then meant Japan. The "Account of the Wa People" in the *Wei Annals* (*Wei Shi, Heren Chuan*), which is part of the famous Chinese historical novel, *The History of the Three Kingdoms* (*San Guo Shi*), describes the life of the Wa people; so does the *History of the Later Han* (*Hou Han Shi*). The country is also referred to as the kingdom of Yamatai, which has been variously identified with the old Yamato Province (around Nara) and Kyushu. These would seem to be the first geographical references to Japan.

Maps of the Age of Explorers

The first Westerner to mention Japan was Marco Polo (ca. 1255–1323). He used the name "Zipangu" or "Cipangu." This is derived from the Chinese "Jih-pen-kuo" (in Japanese, "Nihonkoku," or land of the rising sun). Marco Polo stayed in China with his father Nicolò Polo for seventeen years. He left China in 1292 and got back to Venice in 1295. While imprisoned in Genoa from 1298–99, Marco Polo dictated the account of his travels to one Rusticiano of Pisa. *The Travels of Marco Polo* contains the following description of Zipangu: "Japan [Cipangu] is an island far out to sea to the Eastward some 1,500 miles from the mainland. It is a very big island. The people are fair complexioned, good looking, and well mannered. They are idolators, wholly independent and exercising no authority over any nation but themselves."

He goes on to speak of the palace being roofed in gold, with chambers paved in gold: "They have gold in great abundance, because it is found there in measureless quantities. And I assure you that no one exports it from the island, because no trader, nor indeed anyone else, goes there from the mainland. That is how they come to possess so much of it—so much indeed that I can report to you in sober truth a veritable marvel concerning a certain palace of the ruler of the island. You may take it for a fact that he has a very large palace entirely roofed with fine gold. Just as we roof our houses or churches with lead, so this palace is roofed with fine gold. And the value of it is almost beyond computation. Moreover all the chambers, of which there are many, are likewise paved with fine gold to a depth of more than two fingers' breadth. And the halls and the windows and every other part of the palace are likewise adorned with gold. All in all I can tell you that the palace is of such incalculable richness that any attempt to estimate its value

12

would pass the bounds of the marvellous. They have pearls in abundance, red in colour, very beautiful, large and round. They are worth as much as the white ones, and indeed more. In this island the dead are sometimes buried, sometimes cremated; but everyone who is buried has one of these pearls put in his mouth. Such is the custom that prevails among them. They also have many other precious stones in abundance. It is a very rich island. . . .''

He also gives a fairly full account of Kublai Khan's attempts to invade Japan. It is not perhaps surprising that Marco Polo's picture of Japan should be so misleading, not to say false. He never went there, and Chinese contacts with Japan in the twelfth and thirteenth centuries were, to say the least, exiguous. Moreover, Marco Polo was obviously drawing on his memory some years after he left China, and he, or perhaps Rusticiano, may well have embroidered his story to amuse, excite, or stupefy the medieval reader. In any case, there is nothing to indicate that Marco Polo ever drew any maps. Nevertheless, Marco Polo's account of Japan provided the basis for the inclusion of Japan in European maps from the fourteenth century onward. His false account of Japan's riches in gold may have been due to reports of Japanese roofs made of burnished copper, which can glow like gold. Whatever the case, his description of such fabulous wealth aroused the cupidity of European explorers. It was, indeed, in efforts to reach the gold of Japan that America was discovered.

Japan first appeared on a Western map, the planisphere of Fra Mauro, in 1459, where it was shown as the "Isola de Zimpagu" to the north of Java. Columbus, when he set out on his voyages of discovery, took with him a map showing Cipangu (or Cypango). This was attached to a letter of 1474 from one Paolo Toscanelli to Father Martinez, confessor to the king of Portugal. Unfortunately this map has not survived. Columbus also had a copy of Marco Polo's travels. This has survived, together with Columbus's written notes in the margin. These included such references to Cipangu as "I wish to depart today for the island of Cuba which I do believe is Cipangu. 23 October 1492." He had grossly underestimated the distance to Japan and, in fact, concluded that Spagnola or Espanola (the modern Haiti) was Cypango. As a result of this mistaken belief on the part of Columbus, European cartographers for a time obliterated Japan from their maps of the world, because they could not find any proper place to put it! In 1508 Ruysch, a Dutch cartographer who was active at the beginning of the sixteenth century, concluded that Spagnola was Cypango and wrote: "Therefore we refrain from putting Cypango in addition to Spagnola." In 1526, Franciscus Monarchus even identified Zipangu with the Yucatan in modern Mexico.

Marco Polo's account was the origin of another cartographic error. He had mentioned a land of Ania or Anian lying at the northeast extremity of Asia. This led the Italian cartographer Giacomo Gastaldi (1500–65) to mention, in 1562, a strait of Anian lying between Asia and North America, and the Venetian Bolognino Zallieri (active 1566–70) went so far as to produce a map showing the straits of Anian. Thereafter, the straits of Anian appeared on European maps of Asia for some two centuries. It was only when explorers discovered the true relationship between northeast Asia and America that the imaginary straits of Anian were erased from world maps. The most notable of these explorers was the Danish-Russian traveler Vitus Bering, after whom the Bering Straits were named. Abraham Ortelius's map of 1570 entitled *Tartariae Sive Magni Chami Regni Typus* (Pl.16) shows these imaginary straits very clearly.

The oldest map based on Marco Polo's account of his travels was drawn in Venice, in the Sala dello Scudo of the ducal palace, but this was destroyed by fire in 1483, redrawn by Gastaldi in 1553, damaged again in 1574, and renewed a final time during restorations in 1762. One of the earliest surviving depictions of Japan appeared on the globe of Martin Behaim in 1492. This shows Japan as a very large quadrilateral island with the Tropic of Cancer crossing the northern part of the island (in fact the southernmost tip of Kyushu is about eight degrees north of the Tropic of Cancer). Behaim's depiction of Japan was not, however, the earliest. Henricus Martellus, a German cartographer who was active between 1480 and 1496 and who worked in Florence, appears to have included a map of "Çinpangu Insula" in his *Insularium Illustratum* found in the Biblioteca Laurenziana in Florence, as well as in a world map recently discovered. These maps seem to date from about 1489–90. The depiction

14

is imaginary, but the island shown is similar in outline and location to that of Java Major on fifteenth-century world maps; this confusion underlines the still very hazy ideas about the geography of Asia among European cartographers at this period. Another early depiction of Japan was that of Martin Waldseemüller (1470–1518), a German cartographer, on his world map produced in 1507; he used the name "Zipangri." Eight globe strips, produced in 1515 and attributed to the great Leonardo da Vinci, show an island called "Zipunga," presumably yet another version of the names used for Japan at this time. In these, Japan is shown as a sort of square lying between Asia, South America, and Florida.

In 1528 the Italian cartographer Benedetto Bordone (1460–1531) produced an atlas of islands (*L'Isole del Mondo*, or *Isolario*) printed in Italy by Nicolò d'Aristotle. In it he included a small map of an island which he called "Ciampagu" (Pl.13), presumably another version of Cipangu. This would seem to be the earliest European printed individual map of Japan. Ten years later Gerhardus Mercator placed "Sipango" in the midst of the ocean between the two continents of Asia and North America. Gerhardus Mercator was the Latin name of the famous Flemish cartographer Gerhard Kremer. He lived from 1512 to 1592 and is perhaps best known for the Mercator's projection, which consisted of projecting the meridians on maps as equidistant parallel lines, and latitudes as parallel straight lines at right angles to the meridians.

The first time we find Japan referred to by a name closer in sound to its modern pronunciations than those earlier versions was when the Portuguese Tomé Pires used the word "Jampon" in his *Suma Oriental*, published from 1512 to 1515.* Pires wrote the *Suma* in Malacca, which the Portuguese had reached in 1511. In Malay, Japan was called "Japun" or "Japang," which was also derived from the

---

*Tomé Pires led a Portuguese embassy from Malacca in 1517 with the aim of establishing official commercial relations with China, but he failed to obtain an audience at the Chinese court and was imprisoned in Canton in 1521 because of complaints about Portuguese bad behavior. He eventually died in prison. Meanwhile, a a separate expedition under Jorge Mascarenhas had sailed to explore the Ryukyu Islands to the south of Japan, but this expedition also failed.

Chinese Jih-pen-kuo. Giacomo Gastaldi used the name "Giapan" on a map published in the 1550s.

Japan also seems to have been referred to in the early sixteenth century under the name "Parpoquo Island," perhaps a corruption of Ryukyu, although this seems rather farfetched. A sketch map of about 1515 by Francisco Rodrigues, a Spanish or Portuguese geographer, showed an island shaped like a double wing off the coast of China just north of the present Ryukyu Islands. Parpoquo seems to have been further corrupted to Parioco Insula (also Perioco). This was shown as an island in quadrilateral form, as in Martin Behaim's atlas, in the sea off China in the atlas produced by the Portuguese geographers Lopo Homem and Pedro Reinel in 1519. Although the Portuguese had reached Canton in 1517, they did not come to Japan until some years later, and these early depictions can, therefore, have been based only on hearsay, but the possibilities of trade were tempting and the Portuguese ships were soon roaming the area.

A Portuguese merchant, Fernão Mendes Pinto, claimed in the account of his travels entitled *Peregrinacao* and published after his death in 1614 that he reached Japan in 1542 and was the first European to do so. He wrote that he was a passenger on a Chinese ship which had been blown off course in a gale. He put into the nearest port, which turned out to be that of Tanegashima off the south coast of Kyushu, and traded his cargo. Pinto claimed that he and his two companions, Christovão Borralho and Diogo Zeimoto, were well received by the local daimyo, Tokitaka, who became particularly interested in Zeimoto's arquebus. This was duly presented to the daimyo and later copied by Japanese artisans. Whatever the truth of this story, Japanese firearm manufacture began in Tanegashima. Pinto's claim has been the subject of much dispute. One detractor even went so far as to describe Pinto's account as "a sea of lies with very few islands of truth." Pinto was, however, almost certainly among the first Portuguese to visit Japan, and, in his account, claimed that he visited Japan again in 1546, 1550, and 1554–56. Unfortunately, Pinto's contributions to Portuguese geographical knowledge of Japan were limited, as his book was published only when the Portuguese were about to be expelled from Japan, but he was an effective publicist for his own feats and adventures.

The first confirmed landing by the Portuguese in Japan was in 1543, when three Portuguese seamen, Antonio da Mota, Francisco Zeimoto, and Antonio Peixoto, on their way to Liampo, ran into a storm which forced them onto the coast of Japan at approximately 32° north. They, too, were kindly received by the daimyo of Tanegashima. Japanese documents, in fact, suggest that Portuguese may have visited Japan as early as 1534 and 1539. At any rate, in the late 1540s and 1550s Portuguese voyages to Japan became frequent. In 1547 a momentous meeting took place in Malacca. Fernão Mendes Pinto and a Portuguese sea captain, Jorge Alvares, met the future St. Francis Xavier when Xavier was returning from the Moluccas to India. They gave him a detailed account of what they had seen, and left Xavier "entranced with what he heard of the newly discovered land, and a glorious vista of missionary activity opened up before him." Another early report was that written by Garcia Escalante Alvarado in Lisbon in 1548, addressed to the viceroy of Mexico.

Xavier reached Kagoshima in 1549 and began his missionary activity. In his letters to his Jesuit superiors and to the king of Portugal, he recorded his journeys in Japan. These took him to Kagoshima, Hirado, Yamaguchi, and Miyako (Kyoto). He was no geographer, but place names and descriptions of where he went and of the Japanese people added to geographical knowledge of Japan in Portugal and Rome.

Soon, with the establishment of the Portuguese factory—actually, a trading station or outpost—at Macao in 1557, regular trade missions came to Kyushu, and the cartographers were able to draw on the practical experience of travelers rather than mere hearsay. Eighty Portuguese voyages to Japan were recorded between 1543 and 1590, but as none of the travelers were themselves trained and experienced cartographers, little of the Japanese coastline could be explored by them, and European cartography was still without most of the scientific aids and methods later developed, so it is not surprising that the first maps based on these reports and discoveries were very inaccurate. The geographers' sources were the reports of the

Jesuit fathers who came in the wake of St. Francis Xavier and the Portuguese mariners who brought the trading ships to Japan in the sixteenth century. The fathers tended to concentrate on place names, distances, churches built, and numbers of Japanese converted to Christianity. The mariners, for their part, produced detailed descriptions which might help others to identify routes. Neither the priests nor the mariners appear to have done much in the way of actual mapmaking.

One of the most informative of the Jesuit fathers was Petrus Maffeius. He edited a collection of missionaries' letters which appeared at Louvain in 1569. In these letters, Japan is at first described as a single island, but in 1571 it was reported that there were three main islands, surrounded by other smaller islands. Maffeius recorded that the main island was divided into fifty-three satrapies or kingdoms (*kuni*, or provinces), and that the capital was Meaco, meaning "capital." He referred to a second island as "Ximum" (presumably Kyushu—although the origin of "Ximum" is obscure), with nine satrapies, and a third, "Xiococum" (Shikoku), with four. Japan, he said, lay between 30° and 38° north.

The *roteiros* (English, rutters), which were the navigational notes, or records, of the Portuguese ships (*não*) that visited Japan annually, contained more practical information. The *não* left the Portuguese colony of Goa in India in April or May, wintered at Macao, and left the following May or June with the southwest monsoon for Nagasaki. A journey from Portugal to Japan thus took about two years in those days. They had few nautical instruments, and what they had were simple. Their main instruments were a compass, an astrolabe, and Jacob's staff (a simple instrument for measuring distances and height). They had neither sextant nor telescope. Nor, of course, did they have any accurate chronometers. So, while their readings of latitudes were not far off, their estimates of longitude were little better than guesses. The *roteiros* contained elementary navigational instructions, together with descriptions of coastlines and notes on anchorages, shallows, deep-water areas, prevailing winds, currents, and other nautical phenomena which might help the mariner to find his position. Many of the *roteiros* were, however, very vague or general. Professor Boxer quotes one entry as follows: "In the entry of Nagasaki there is nothing

18

else to do, than only to run in through the middle thereof, till you be in the road, where you must anchor.'' These fairly obvious instructions could hardly have been much help.

In the second half of the sixteenth century, the Low Countries became the main center of European mapmaking, as the Dutch began to take over from the Portuguese and the Spaniards as merchant adventurers in the Far East. The British came onto the Far Eastern scene rather later and, after their brief and unsuccessful effort at Hirado in the early seventeenth century, concentrated on the trade with India. Moreover, in mapmaking, despite great names like Saxton and Speed, London never challenged Antwerp and Amsterdam as a center of world cartography. One factor in the development of cartography in the Netherlands was probably the Spanish dominion there, and the possibility this gave for the transfer of the results of Iberian discoveries to the Netherlands. But the Portuguese and Spaniards were secretive about the geographical information they collected, and they remained bitter rivals in Japan and elsewhere despite the unification of the kingdoms of Portugal and Spain in 1581. Moreover, the Dutch and the Flemings hated their Iberian rulers, and by 1581 the Northern Netherlands were already in revolt (the revolt had begun as early as 1566). Nevertheless, it was at Antwerp and Amsterdam that Mercator, Ortelius, de Jode, and Hondius established the foundations of modern European cartography.

A number of attempts have been made to classify the various depictions of Japan on sixteenth-century maps. E.W. Dahlgren, for instance, in his work, *Les Débuts de la Cartographie du Japon*, divides them into six main types named after representative mapmakers. Armando Cortesão, in his colossal study of early Portuguese mapmaking, includes forty-nine diagams showing the evolution of the depiction of Japan from Martin Behaim in 1492 to a map of 1649. He prefers to divide the early maps into seven groups. However, it may be helpful to the general reader to set out the sixteenth-century types of maps of Japan on the basis of the shapes used for Japan. These may be summarized as follows:

1. A single, rectangular island, generally drawn north to south, sometimes with a number of small islands around, based solely on hearsay (usually Marco Polo),

without any connections with reality—except by luck. One example is that of Martin Behaim (see p. 14). Bordone's map of 1528 and Münster's of 1540 fall into this category.

2. A single island with a few smaller islands nearby, generally drawn horizontally west to east (Pl. 14). Armando Cortesão calls this the Gastaldi type and says that it was based on information contained in a letter written by St. Francis Xavier in Kagoshima in 1549 and sent to Rome. A map by Paolo Furlani of 1574 and another by Joan Martines of 1589 belong to this group. In fact, they show little if any progress over the first type.

3. Two rows of islands leading to the northeast from the Ryukyu Islands. This is found in two charts and was apparently based on information from the first Portuguese visits to Japan. The first (ca. 1550) is anonymous; the second is ascribed to one Sancho Gutièrrez (flourished 1551–61).

4. A number of islands, including one fairly large one, shown as an extension of the Korean peninsula (Pl. 15). Cortesão ascribes this type to Lopo Homem (1497–1572); Dahlgren preferred to call it after Diogo Homem, who was active between 1530 and 1576.

5. One large island, either round or oval, with small islands to the north and south as in Mercator's map of 1569 or as in Ortelius's *Indiae Orientalis Insularumque Adiacientium Typus* of 1570 (Pl. 17). Ortelius was the Latin name of another Flemish cartographer, Abraham Wortels, who was born at Antwerp in 1527 and lived until 1598. His *Theatrum Orbis Terrarum* was one of the first great atlases of the world. In 1575 he was appointed geographer to King Philip II of Spain, thus helping to ensure that Iberian cartographic knowledge spread to the Low Countries.

6. Four islands (the largest corresponding to Honshu) set out north to south, thus including what may have been intended to be Ezo, the modern Hokkaido. This depiction is found in the charts of Bartolomeu Velho (Pl. 18), who was active between 1560 and 1568.

7. One main north-south island with a series of small islands to the south and an island called Tonsa to the east, as in Ortelius's *Asiae Nova Descriptio* of 1567 (Pl. 19),

or one main island east-west, with a series of small islands to the southwest, and the island of Tonsa to the south, as in Ortelius's *Tartariae Sive Magni Chami Regni Typus*, also of 1570. The name Tonsa is derived from Tosa, the province on the south side of Shikoku, now Kōchi Prefecture. The name Tonsa was used by European cartographers for Shikoku into the eighteenth century.

8. Three main islands, with Honshu shown as lying east-west but with the western end turned southward. Kyushu is shown lying north-south, and Shikoku east-west, almost as if it were an island in a large gulf between Kyushu and the southern tip of eastern Honshu. The first map of this type was drawn by one Lazaro Luiz in 1563, and the second by Fernão Vaz Dourado in 1568 (Pl. 20). Nothing seems to be known about the life of Vaz Dourado except that he was for a time in Goa and his maps of 1568 and 1571 are dated from Goa. Ortelius also produced a map of this type in 1584.

Another interesting example of this last type by Ortelius is his *Maris Pacifici Novissima Descriptio* of 1589 (Pl. 21), which shows a large island called "Isla de Plata" to the north of Honshu. Perhaps this was intended as a depiction of Ezo, or Hokkaido. Jan Huygen Van Linschóten, a Dutch cartographer who lived from 1563 to 1610, also produced a map of this type which was widely used. His collection of marine maps of the world was published at Amsterdam by Cornelius Claeszon. These were based at least partly on the work of Petrius Plancius (1552–1622), another Dutch cartographer, and Bartolomeo de Lasso. Both were cartographers to the king of Spain. He also obtained information from his friend Dirck Gerritsz, who had spent twenty-six years in India. The map of East Asia in Linschóten's work (Pl. 22) was drawn by Arnoldus à Langren, or Arnold van Langren, another Dutch cartographer, and was based on the knowledge of Portuguese mariners. Linschóten's account of Japan in the first part of his book is brief; he says that Japan lies between 30° and 38° north, and he refers to "Nangasache" (Nagasaki), but says little else. The second part, which consists of an account of voyages of Portuguese mariners in the East (*Reysgeschrifft van de Navigatien der Portugal Oysers in Orienten*), contains more of interest about Japan. The most important part consists of sailing instructions from Macao and Liampo to Bungo,

Nangasaque (Nagasaki), Firando (Hirado), and Arima in Kyushu. Chapter 31 gives an account of the sea around Shikoku as far as Saquay (Sakai, the port of Osaka). The south coast of Honshu between Caminaziqqe (Kaminoseki) and Sakai is also described. Many of the place names given are now difficult to identify, and some of the distances given are inaccurate, but the position of Shikoku is approximately correct, although only two harbors are named. The largest part is devoted to Kyushu. Detailed advice is given about the approaches to various harbors, together with advice about routes in case of typhoons. Linschóten's work was reproduced in Dutch, English, Latin, and French editions. Although, as Professor Boxer has pointed out, Linschoten's maps on a scale of 1:12.5 million and those of other sixteenth-century cartographers were completely useless as practical charts for mariners, manuals accompanying the maps were an essential standby for the navigators of the time. Captain John Saris, in his journal recording his return voyage from Japan in the Clove in 1613–14, noted that ''wee found Ian Huijghen Van Linschotens booke very true, for thereby we directed our selues from our setting forth from Firando.''

Thus far European maps of Japan had been generally fanciful and very inaccurate, although as the information came in from the missionaries and mariners the depiction improved and more names, even if corrupt, were included. It was only towards the end of the century, when knowledge of Japan had greatly increased and Gyōgi-type maps had almost certainly become available, that European printed maps of Japan with some resemblance to reality appeared. The Europeans in the sixteenth century fixed the southern latitudes of the country with reasonable accuracy, but they were vague and inaccurate in their estimates of the longitude of the Japanese islands, as well as of the latitude of the northern part of Japan.

It was because of the increasing cross-fertilization of European and Japanese cultures that the final years of the sixteenth century and the first few years of the seventeenth century were particularly significant in the history of Japanese maps. In Europe cartography had improved, and knowledge of Japan had greatly increased with the development of contacts not only between Japan and Portugal but also with Spain and, later, the Netherlands. At the same time, in Japan European cartography began to exercise an influence on Japanese cartography, although, as we have already seen, Gyōgi-type maps continued to be used, if only for decorative purposes, right down to the nineteenth century.

An important source for European cartographers in the final decade of the sixteenth century was the reports of the Portuguese traveler Ignacio Moreira, who was in Japan from 1590 to 1592 working with the Jesuits, although not himself a member of the order. Moreira, who came to Japan with Valignano, the Jesuit Visitor, traveled with him from Nagasaki to Kyoto and Nagoya when Valignano called on Toyotomi Hideyoshi as ambassador of the Portuguese viceroy of India. During these journeys he recorded latitudes and other geographical information. He also produced a new and independent map of Japan. Unfortunately, although the explanation of Moreira's map is preserved in the archives of the Society of Jesus, no authenticated copy of the map has been found.

Another source seems to have been Gyōgi-type maps which found their way to Europe in the final decades of the century. Two such maps have been discovered. One, at least, seems to date from the mission of the young Japanese nobles which Valignano arranged in 1582. During the course of their travels from Portugal through Spain and Italy, they went to Florence and may there have given a map, perhaps as an explanation of their country, to the Grand Duke of Tuscany, Francisco I (Primo) de Medici. At any rate, in 1931 a map entitled "Japam" (Pl. 23) was discovered among the Medici papers dealing with the East Indian trade by Professor G. Crino of the University of Florence. The map is anonymous and has no date or place of origin, but the nature of the map, which is a primitive copy of a Gyōgi-type map, suggests that it may have been made by a Portuguese who acted as interpreter to the mission. Only twenty-six out of the sixty-six provinces of Japan are named. On the southern 'margin there is a reference to a land "where there are no men, only women, and men who go there are massacred." This is clearly a reference to Rasetsukoku (see pp. 6–7). Yehogaxima (Ezo, or Hokkaido) is named, but the island is not shown. Only three places are named: Meaco (Kyoto), Sacai (Sakai), and Azuchi. Azuchi castle was built in 1576 and the donjon (*tenshukaku*) was burned down in June 1582 when Oda

Nobunaga, the military ruler before Toyotomi Hideyoshi, was murdered. Valignano left Japan on February 20, 1582, without knowing of the destruction of Azuchi castle and the murder of Oda Nobunaga. This tends to confirm both the date and origin of the map.

Another Gyōgi-type map has been found in the Arquivo Historico Nacional in Madrid. This is a very primitive sketch. It is dated 1587 and was contained in a fourteen-page report on a mission sent in 1585–86 by the daimyo of Hirado, Matsuura Hizen no Kami (governor of the province of Hizen), to Santiago de Vera, then the Spanish viceroy of the Philippines.

A further source may well have been Chinese printed maps. The Chinese and the Koreans had used Gyōgi-type maps when depicting Japan (see p. 8), and it is generally accepted that Chinese maps of China had a considerable influence on European maps of China. A Chinese map entitled *Gujin Xing Sheng Zhi Tu* in a 1555 edition has been preserved in the general archives of the Indies in Seville. This shows Japan as a long, generally oblong island to the south of the Korean peninsula.

The earliest printed individual map of Japan (if we leave aside Bordone's fanciful depiction) was published in 1586 in Renwart Cysat's *Wahrhafftiger Bericht* (True Report) in Freyburg in Switzerland. This shows the outline of Japan (Pl. 24; the shape owes something to the Gyōgi-type maps) and indicates the seminaries and novitiate of the Jesuit order in Japan. The world map of 1589 by Urbano Monti also indicated that knowledge of Japan was spreading, as he claimed to have made use of information obtained through Valignano and the "embassy" of young Japanese nobles who were visiting Europe, including Italy, in 1585. The size of Japan is greatly exaggerated, filling almost all of the northern part of the Pacific between China and North America, and the Japanese islands are shown in peculiar form.

However, the really significant European map of Japan of this time was that by Luis Teixeira, a Jesuit (Father Ludovico Teixeira, or Tesseira). We know that this map (Pl. 25) was prepared in about 1592, as it was enclosed with a letter which Teixeira sent to Ortelius dated February 20, 1592. The map, entitled *Iaponiae Insulae Descriptio*, appeared as an addendum to Ortelius' atlas, *Theatrum Orbis Terrarum*, published in 1595. Luis Teixeira, who was the son of Pedro Fernandes, the founder of a large family of cartographers, had been appointed cartographer to the Spanish crown in 1569 and is also known for his work on the Azores. As far as we know, he never went East, let alone to Japan.

Teixeira's map, which was reprinted and copied over the next fifty to sixty years, represented a landmark in the cartography of Japan, and many subsequent European maps of Japan owed at least something to Teixeira. The map is distinguished by its depiction of Japan as three main islands with Honshu running broadly east and west, a more realistic if still inaccurate depiction of Kyushu, called Bungo after the province of that name, and an improved outline of Shikoku, called Tonsa, although the Bay of Tosa is not shown, and the Inland Sea is much too broad. The eastern end of Honshu is stunted, and Ezo, or Hokkaido, is not shown, while Korea is shown as a long island with an elongated point. The cartouche is elegant, and three sailing ships are shown (two off the coast of China, one to the south of Shikoku).

The map was copied in the Mercator-Hondius atlas of 1606 with minor modifications and entitled *Iaponia* (Pl. 26). The cartouches are different, as are the sailing ships, which have been reduced in number to two. An ornamental dolphin is depicted south of Korea, on which there is a brief note in Latin to the effect that in war the Koreans are energetic, but cruel and barbarous. Mercator produced a minature version in his *Atlas Minor* of 1607. Jan Jansson (1596–1664) produced yet another version in 1647, under the title *Iaponiae Nova Descriptio* (Pl. 27), with minor variations to the cartouches and the decoration—the two sailing ships have been altered, and the dolphin on the left is shown partly submerged. The maps were accompanied by texts describing Japan in Latin or the language of the country of publication.

European Influences on Japanese Maps

It is much easier to trace the influence of European maps on Japanese cartography. The young nobles, representing the daimyo of Bungo, Arima, and Ōmura in Kyushu, who were sent by Father Valignano as an "embassy" to Europe received various presents during their stay in Portugal, Spain, and Italy. When they visited Padua they are reported to have been given a copy of Ortelius's celebrated atlas, *Theatrum Orbis Terrarum*, which they brought back to Japan. Other atlases were brought to Japan by the Jesuit missionaries. We also have records showing that the English sent maps. For instance, the cargo of the Thomas, which reached Hirado on June 20, 1616, included not only maps of British counties, Britain, and London, but also a world map and two globes.

The Japanese also had access to the map of the world which the famous Jesuit missionary in China, Father Matteo Ricci, published in China in 1600. As it was written in Chinese, it was not censored in the same way as European books and manuscripts were during and after the seventeenth-century Japanese persecutions of the Christians. This formed the basis of the first world map printed in Japan, in 1645, under the title *Bankoku Sōzu* (General Map of the World). Ricci's map of the world put China, the "Middle Kingodm," in the center; the Japanese, perhaps because Japan was not generally in the center of European world maps at this time, seem to have followed the European rather than the Chinese model, although in later maps of the world produced in Japan, Japan is more centrally located.

European maps of the world in fact became the basis of a number of maps of the world which were painted on screens during the latter part of the sixteenth and the early seventeenth centuries and which seem to have had quite a vogue during this period. Some twenty screen maps have survived natural disasters and wars and have been preserved, brilliant reminders of the glories of Momoyama painting. World screen maps such as those at the Jōtoku-ji in Fukui (Pls.35, 36) as well as those in other Japanese collections were generally painted in a number of colors on sixfold screens with gold surrounds. In the Jōtoku-ji world-map screen, the world is more accurately depicted than in some later Japanese world maps, and Japan is shown on the far right.

When the Japanese came to depict their own country at this period, they followed

Gyōgi-type maps rather than European models, but perhaps under European influence, or equally probably because of a greater knowledge of their own country and cartography, they began to make significant improvements in the Gyōgi-type depiction. The screens with world maps were generally accompanied by parallel screens showing a map of Japan only. Probably the earliest, and certainly one of the most striking and artistically important of these pairs of maps, is the pair preserved in the Jōtoku-ji. These screens have been ascribed to the great painter Kanō Eitoku (1543–90). If so, they must have been painted before 1590, but although Eitoku's seal was used, experts doubt whether they are really his work. However, the map of Japan includes geographical information relevant to Toyotomi Hideyoshi's campaigns against Korea in 1592 and 1597. For instance, the line followed by the expeditions to Korea from Kyushu via the island of Tsushima is shown. Thus, the screens would almost certainly seem to have been painted before the turn of the century. Kyushu is much more accurately depicted than in the usual Gyōgi-type map. The tip of Ezo (Hokkaido) is shown and the Japanese coastline is more accurately depicted, even if some Gyōgi-type aberrations such as exaggerating the size of the Bōsō Peninsula (at the southern tip of present-day Chiba Prefecture) and the Nōtō Peninsula (in present-day Ishikawa Prefecture) have been retained. Mount Fuji and a chain of mountains in Tōhoku are shown in pictorial form.

The other screens which have survived show interesting variations, although the convention of surrounding Japan in golden clouds seems to have been generally followed. The magnificent pair of screens (Pls. 32, 33) preserved in the Namban Museum at Osaka, with the surrounding panels to the world map showing different peoples of the world in their various costumes, real or imaginary, is particularly interesting. This follows a European tradition that can be seen in the maps of such cartographers as the Dutch Blaeu and the English Speed (see Pl. 29).

During this period the Japanese also began to develop their own navigational charts. They had, we can assume, got hold of some Portuguese charts, although as we have seen these were not much use for detailed navigation. They also had access to Dutch charts. Maritime charts signed by the Dutch cartographer Cornelius

Doedtsz, apparently drawn at Edam, Holland, probably came into Japanese hands after the wreck in 1600 of the Dutch ship Liefde on which William Adams was the master pilot. These charts, now in the Ueno Museum, apparently came from the Tokugawa archives in 1868. Professor Charles Boxer has suggested that these might have included "the chart of the whole world" which Adams showed to Tokugawa Ieyasu (1542–1616) when the latter asked him how he had come to Japan.

Japanese seamen began to make illegal trading voyages to Korea and China as early as the middle of the twelfth century. After the failure of the Mongol attempts to invade Japan in the late thirteenth century, Japanese seamen came increasingly to operate as ruthless and tough pirates, ravaging the Chinese coast at various times during the Ming dynasty (1368–1661). To halt these depredations, the Ming court established diplomatic relations with the Ashikaga shogunate, and trading ships called *kangobune* (literally, "tally ships") were officially authorized, the first dating from 1404. Later, in the fifteenth century, the Ming court prohibited Japanese traders from entering Chinese ports, but the rules were not strictly enforced and piracy grew until it was suppressed in 1563 and 1564 by the Chinese viceroy, Yue Tai-yau. This action forced the Japanese seamen to seek new areas of operation, including Formosa, Luzon, and Annam. During the early years the Japanese pilots appear to have relied almost entirely on notes of earlier voyages and oral traditions. At any rate, no maps or charts from this period have survived.

Toyotomi Hideyoshi, unlike some earlier rulers and the successors of Tokugawa Ieyasu, encouraged foreign trade and established a system of licensed trading ships, known as *goshuinsen*. Eight wealthy merchants (three from Kyoto, one from Sakai, and four from Nagasaki) were granted licenses by the shogunate. Ieyasu for his part also recognized the value of foreign trade and sent more than a dozen ships each year to trade with Formosa, South China, Indochina, the Philippines, Siam (Thailand), Malacca, and Borneo. This trade continued until the policy of seclusion was adopted in the 1630s. Many of the Japanese merchants who went on these voyages set up local Japanese communities which were even able to continue, for a time at least, after all communications with their homeland were cut off. At first ships probably used Portuguese charts, but they must later have developed their own charts. Unfortunately, as part of the seclusion policy, the Tokugawa shogunate destroyed all the data about these ships, except for some documents covering the period from 1604 to 1616 preserved by the Nanzen-ji in Kyoto. Even less material on the maps and charts has survived. No more than twenty documents have been preserved, and all the maps are anonymous because the men who drew them were sailors employed by the shipowners and not officially recognized cartographers or professional men. Two charts which have been preserved show the wide area covered by Japanese traders. One Sueyoshi Magozaemon (1570–1617) obtained a license to trade with Luzon in the Philippines, Siam, and Annam (Indochina), but he never visited any of these places. His chart on vellum is still kept by his descendants in Osaka. Another chart on vellum, which was sent home to Matsuzaka (now in Mie Prefecture) by a Japanese merchant ship, is said to have been used between 1631 and 1636 by Kadoya Shichirōbei, who lived in Cacciam (Quinan) in Annam and was the ruler of the local Japanese community, where he apparently married a "native princess." These charts were drawn on the basis of Portuguese charts of the mid-sixteenth century, except that Japan, Korea, and Formosa were drawn on the basis of Japanese knowledge of these places. The depiction is, as a result, considerably more accurate than on contemporary European maps. It was indeed a great deal better than in Japanese maps made in the latter part of the seventeenth century and the first half of the eighteenth century. Professor Hiroshi Nakamura, a scholar of Japanese cartography, says that the Portuguese-style Japanese charts were drawn following the Portuguese style of mapmaking by determining the geographical position of a place from astronomical observation. He adds that the general depiction of Japan "cannot be distinguished by non-professional eyes from that in the maps of Inō Tadataka (1745–1818), who drew them after eighteen years of assiduous surveying of the Japanese coasts." The Japanese once again showed their capacity for imitation and improvement, but as a result of the isolationist policies of the Tokugawa shogunate, the knowledge gained was soon lost and had to be relearned with effort and difficulty towards the end of the eighteenth century.

The Years of Isolation

Japanese Mapmaking in the Tokugawa Period

For some 250 years Japan was almost totally closed to the Western world. The only loophole was through the tiny Dutch merchant community at Deshima in Nagasaki. At first there was not much wish to learn from the foreigners, who were despised not merely for what the Japanese regarded as their uncouth manners, but also because they were engaged in trade. In the Japanese social hierarchy the merchants came at the bottom of the pile, after the artisans and the farmers, and naturally far below the samurai. Gradually, however, some enlightened Japanese scholars began to recognize that especially in the field of science they had much to learn from the "red-haired barbarians," and the so-called Dutch studies, or *Rangaku*, were developed. Surveying and cartography played a minor part in these and had some influence on the development of Japanese mapmaking. But a good deal had to be improvised by the Japanese without adequate knowledge of Western cartographical methods. It is a tribute to men like Inō Tadataka that they in the end achieved so much.

The effort put into the making of maps during these centuries reflected the nature and development of Japanese society and economy during the years of seclusion. The first and perhaps most significant achievement of the Tokugawa shogunate was the establishment of internal peace and order. This was done through the creation of a new feudal structure. Many of the old daimyo—at least those who had good sense or good fortune to side with the Tokugawa after the death of Toyotomi Hideyoshi—were left in possession of their fiefs or parts of them, or were transferred to other fiefs. The Tokugawa, however, took care to insure that these daimyo, who became known as the *tozama* or "outer" daimyo, were kept under observation and discouraged from rebelling by the allocation of neighboring fiefs to daimyo with kinship or other close ties to the Tokugawa. These *fudai* daimyo (hereditary vassals), many of whom were given or adopted the name of Matsudaira, were allocated some of the best lands in the country. The daimyo were also kept in order by the *sankinkōtai* system. This was a law enacted in 1634 by the third shogun, Iemitsu, which obliged the daimyo to spend half their lives in Edo and, when they returned to their fiefs, to leave their wives and children behind as hostages. The time of residence in Edo was not fixed on any absolute basis, but most daimyo remained one year at Edo and one in their fiefs. Daimyo with fiefs near Edo, however, used to alternate every six months.

Peace made it possible for the towns to grow, while the existence of a landed aristocracy with no wars to fight created a demand for the services of craftsmen and merchants. Agriculture also developed to supply the towns with food and to provide the daimyo with the funds they needed to maintain their positions, and thus the demands for goods and services expanded. Rigidity and the failure to adapt and innovate were the seeds of the decline which hit the system in the latter part of the era, but the earlier years of prosperity and peace provided a major stimulus to the development of Japanese mapmaking.

The first demand for maps was the same as in ancient times—to define the estates or fiefs and show their interrelationship with one another. With this was coupled the need for maps to enable the centralized regime established by the Tokugawa to operate reasonably efficiently and in particular to insure that peace and order were maintained The shogunate instituted the office of *metsuke* (literally, "watcher") to survey the activities of the daimyo and the lesser officials. These *metsuke*, who were in effect official inspectors, censors, and even perhaps spies, could hardly do without at least improvised maps. Maps were also, of course, required for the regular journeys which the daimyo had to undertake to and from Edo. The great routes of Japan were developed with regular stages and networks of inns and post houses. Roads were built and marked by pines along their borders, and barriers (*sekisho*) established so that the traffic could be regulated—especially to prevent the smuggling of arms into Edo and hostages out. Fording places had to be marked, and where the rivers were not too broad or swift-flowing in the rainy season, bridges built.

The Tokugawa shogunate lost no time in making sure of their control of the country and of the taxes they needed for this purpose. In 1603 it issued its first instructions to the daimyo to make maps of their domains (Pl. 31). These maps were assembled and the resulting map of Japan (Pl. 30) on a scale of 1:280,000 has been preserved in the National Diet Library. The map has a number of deficiencies. The Tōhoku region is compressed, the eastern coast of the Bōsō Peninsula is drawn as if it were straight, and the Bay of Tosa in Shikoku is not shown. However, the map is an improvement on that depicted on the Jōtoku-ji screen and the scale is, of course, much larger.

A second series of maps was commissioned in 1644 during the reign of Iemitsu, the third Tokugawa shogun. This was needed because various changes had occurred in the fiefs. For this survey the scale was fixed in advance at 1:21,600. The resulting map was very large. The coastline on this occasion may, it is thought, have reflected the survey made in 1611 by the Spanish mariner Vizcaino. Sebastian Vizcaino had been sent by the Spanish viceroy of Mexico as leader of a mission to Japan. He left Vera Cruz on March 22, 1611, on board the San Francisco with the aim of discovering the "gold and silver" islands to the east of Japan (Marco Polo's false story would not lie down), and of undertaking a survey which would make safer the voyage of Spanish ships from the Philippines to Mexico. He had on board some Japanese merchants who had traveled to Mexico in one of the ships which Adams had built and which had been lent to Don Rodrigo de Vivero y Velasco after he was shipwrecked in Japan in 1609 (Vivero left Japan in August 1610).

Vizcaino sighted the Japanese coast not far from Mito. He landed at Uraga and visited Ieyasu at Suruga (Shizuoka). The Spaniards had permission to survey the whole coast from Nagasaki to Akita, but although Vizcaino is recorded as having explored a good deal from Sendai in Tōhoku to the south, neither of the maps which he drew nor the *roteiro* of the voyage has survived.

The Japanese began at this time to gain some knowledge of Western methods of surveying. One Higuchi Gonemon of Nagasaki studied the subject under a Dutchman some time between 1624 and 1648. Higuchi then taught European methods of surveying, and his pupils established various schools of land surveying. One of them in 1687 produced a thesis on the subject, but they had not learned enough to master the subject, and their contribution to Japanese cartography was accordingly limited.

During this period the Japanese cartographer Hōjō Ujinaga (1610–70) apparently learned some of the principles of geometry and surveying from a Dutch gunner called Juriaen Schaedel, who with three other companions was employed at Edo by the shogun's government for about nine months in 1650 to give lessons in mathematics, gunnery, surveying, and other disciplines. In view of the broad range of the subjects Schaedel was engaged in teaching, it is not surprising that Hōjō Ujinaga, who compiled a map of Japan on the scale of 1:432,000, did not penetrate very far into the subject and did not learn any theory of map projection. As a result, his maps continued to be as generally inaccurate as those of most of his contemporaries.

Despite these studies and the number of charts, maps, atlases, and globes which the Dutch continued to bring to Japan, the third series of fief maps ordered by the shogun Tsunayoshi in 1697, following a decline in revenue, were even less accurate than the earlier series.

However inaccurate they were, printed maps became increasingly popular with the development of woodblock printing. This was also the era in which the print artists began to flourish. They soon recognized the demand for cheap maps for travelers, both daimyo and merchants, and applied their artistic talents to the production of attractive as well as informative maps (Pl. 37). Nakabayashi Kichibei, who was active as a printer of maps in Kyoto, brought out in 1666 a map of Japan entitled *Fusōkoku no Zu* (Map of the Land of the Rising Sun, Pl. 38). While this included some details not found on earlier Gyōgi-type maps, it failed to reflect the progress made by the Tokugawa surveys. Rasetsukoku to the south and Gandō to the north are still on the map and Tōhoku remains vastly foreshortened and apparently largely unknown. To the east of Tōhoku, Matsumae is shown as part of the land going off the map to the north and east and extending south to a latitude below that of Edo. Eight ships are depicted in various waters around Japan.

The greatest mapmaker of the time was Ishikawa Ryūsen (flourished 1688–1713), who was a disciple of the famous ukiyo-e artist Hishikawa Moronobu. His best-known map was first published in 1687 under the title *Honchō Zukan Kōmoku* (An Outline Map of Japan, Pl. 44). This was large in format and included the names of important places on the main routes. It and other contemporary maps (Pl. 39) showed not only the individual provinces, but also the number of *koku* (1 *koku* is 5.119 U.S. bushels) of rice which each daimyo received from his fief. There were also references to castle towns, important scenic spots and routes, as well as useful information for the traveler. Many copies and revisions were produced down to the end of the eighteenth century. Although informative and artistically attractive, the shape of the land was distorted for decorative reasons and topographically inaccurate. Japan is depicted as lying basically east-west. Tōhoku was compressed and bears little relation to the real shape of the area. Kujukurihama (a beach in modern Chiba Prefecture) is shown as if the coast were deeply indented. The Izu and Miura peninsulas are depicted as roughly equivalent in their southward inclination.

In 1719 yet another survey was ordered by the eighth shogun, Yoshimune. One Takebe Katahiro took readings from mountains and produced a map of a scale of 1:216,000. This corrected many of the errors of the previous series, but Japanese methods of cartography were still primitive, and his map remained comparatively inaccurate. A group of cartographers had also developed in rivalry with Ryūsen and other Kyoto mapmakers. Mabuchi Jikōan collaborated with Okada Jiseikan (also called Keishi, and the author of a nineteen-volume book of geographical descriptions) to produce maps which were entitled "revised" or "amended," suggesting that they were better than Ryūsen's. One map of 1703 was called the *Kaisei Dainihon Zenzu* (Revised Map of Great Japan, Pl. 40). On this map Tōhoku is indeed more accurately shown than in Ryūsen's maps, as it is depicted slanting north, and the Bay of Tosa is shown; but in general the map is neither as informative nor as decorative as Ryūsen's.

34

The next major advance came toward the end of the eighteenth century with Nagakubo Sekisui (active from 1770 onward), who was a Confucian scholar from Mito. Mito was the center of the Mito branch of the Tokugawa and was famous for its Confucian scholarship. Nagakubo's map, the *Kaisei Nihon Yochirō Teizenzu* (Revised Map of all Japan And its Main Routes, Pl. 41), which was frequently reprinted and revised, first appeared in 1779. He used the fairly small scale of 1:1,296,000, but his maps were considerably more accurate than those of his predecessors. Although his readings of longitude were inaccurate, as his knowledge of astronomy was limited, his were the first Japanese maps to use longitudinal lines.

Nagakubo Sekisui was the forerunner of probably the greatest Japanese cartographer, Inō Tadataka, who indeed has a claim to world recognition. Inō Tadataka was born in what is now Chiba Prefecture, and his home at Sahara has been preserved as a museum. He spent the first part of his life working as a sakè brewer, only retiring from business when he was fifty. He then went to Edo, where he began to study astronomy and surveying under Takahashi Yoshitoki (1764–1804; also known as Sakuza-emon), an eminent astronomer nineteen years his junior. Takahashi and Inō were particularly interested in determining the length of one degree of latitude and for this purpose sought permission to survey the coast of Ezo, at a time when maps were urgently needed because of the possible Russian threat to the northern islands. This survey lasted from June until November 1800. Mamiya Rinzō (1780–1845), who studied astronomy and surveying under Inō, later usefully supplemented Inō's survey of Ezo. In 1801, Inō began work on the eastern coast of Honshu, from which he continued on to the Japan Sea coast. Gradually he covered the whole of Japan and his survey was completed in 1816. He then began the task of turning the results into maps. This was not completed at the time of his death in May 1818, but his pupils eventually concluded his work and the results were presented to the authorities at the end of September, 1821.

Inō determined the length of one degree of latitude to be 28.2 *ri*, or 110.85 kilometers, which is very nearly accurate (according to the so-called Bessel constants the mean length of one degree of the meridian between 35° and 41° is 110.98 kilometers—a difference of about 1/1000th of a degree). He produced 214 maps on a large scale of 1:36,000, eight maps on a medium scale of 1:216,00, and three maps on the scale of 1:432,000. One of Inō's maps, *Nishi Nihon* (Western Japan), can be seen in Plate 45. The coastline and roads were accurately surveyed and place names carefully recorded, but hills were mostly depicted in profile in dark green. Rivers were recorded in blue, and the coast was bordered by light blue, while azimuth lines to prominent peaks were drawn in red. His instruments were constructed to his own and his colleagues' designs. Magnetic compasses, magnetic theodolites, quadrants, and the perambulator used to compute distances by the number of revolutions of the wheel were carefully constructed and can be seen in the Inō Museum. His method of survey, that of the traverse, was the method in general use at that time. His maps were drawn on the sinusoidal graticule with Kyoto, Nishisanjō as his meridian, or zero. (Nishisanjō was the location of the calendaric office in Kyoto; in his earlier maps he used his house in Kuroe-chō in Edo as meridian. Greenwich did not become accepted internationally as zero until 1884). The sinusoidal projection is an equal-area representation of the surface of the earth having a straight equator and a straight central meridian that is one half of the equator's length. The other lines of longitude are curved. The lines of latitude are straight, and parallel to the equator. This is also known to cartographers as the Sanson-Flamsteed method. It was probably first used in a map of South America added to the Mercator-Hondius atlas of 1606. It was also used by the cartographer Nicolas Sanson d'Abbeville in his world atlas of 1650. The method was named for the English astronomer John Flamsteed (1646–1719), who first developed it. It was not, however, used in European maps of Japan, and we have no evidence that Inō came into direct contact with maps using this method of projection, or with Western works on surveying. Inō must, however, almost certainly have seen manuals on surveying produced by the Jesuits in China and translated into Chinese during the first half of the eighteenth century. Being in Chinese, they were exempt from the general Tokugawa ban on foreign publications. In any case it seems certain that Inō learned the principles of mapmaking and developed his instruments

36

on the basis of instructions from Takahashi Yoshitoki. Professor Ryōkichi Ōtani has suggested in his book on Inō Tadataka that the reason why Inō adopted this method of projection was because it was simple to draw and convenient. Takahashi later devised a more accurate method of projection, but in order to complete his survey quickly Inō did not adopt this method. Professor Ōtani concluded that Inō was responsible for the "improper adjustment and compilation" of the map of the eastern half of Japan; but for the great mistakes in projecting the complete map of Japan, Takahashi Kageyasu (1785–1829), Yoshitoki's son, was principally responsible.

Copies of Inō's survey were reproduced even after the Meiji Restoration in 1868 and were highly regarded by Western cartographers, including those from the Royal Navy in the latter part of the nineteenth century, despite errors in calculation. While Inō's determinations of latitude by astronomical observation were remarkably accurate, he did not determine longitudes astronomically because he had no accurate lunar table and his instruments were inadequate. Instead he obtained longitudinal locations geodetically.

In 1861 HMS Acteon and three gunboats reached Nagasaki to undertake surveys of the Japanese coast. Rutherford Alcock, the British Minister, requested the help of the Japanese authorities, who duly supplied officials to serve on the ships. They took with them a copy, in three sheets, of the smallest of the maps prepared from Inō's survey. Alcock reported to the Foreign Office in London that Commander Ward, the Captain of HMS Acteon "has carefully . . . . compared these [i.e. Inō's] with some of his own surveys and although they have been made without our instruments and astronomical observations he is delighted to find they are so accurate that they may be trusted and thus avoid many of the difficulties Your Excellencies feared might result."

Japanese maps during the Tokugawa period did not consist simply of maps of Japan. Despite the ban on foreign intercourse, the shogun's government could not totally suppress interest in the outside world, and various world maps were produced, including the famous *Bankoku Sōzu* (Pl. 42) of 1645, now in the Kobe City Museum, which was based on the world map produced in China by the Jesuit missionary

Matteo Ricci and which was accompanied by attractive depictions of the natives of various parts of the world (Pl. 43).

Professor Shintarō Ayusawa, in a study of "the types of world maps made in Japan's age of national isolation," divides these maps into the following five types:

1. "Objective" world maps were those based on foreign originals. They include the *Bankoku Sōzu*, and the *Shintei Bankoku Zenzu* (New Universal Map) produced by the shogun's astronomer, Takahashi Kageyasu. Other interesting—and surprisingly inaccurate—examples are on view in Plates 46 and 47.

2. World maps representing Buddhist cosmology. Ayusawa says that the first of these, entitled *Nansembushū Bankoku Shōka no Zu* (World Map, Pl. 48), was drawn by a Buddhist priest called Rōkashi and published in 1710. It became the prototype of other Buddhist world maps (Pl. 49). These maps, which show an imaginary India at the heart of the world, confuse the real world with the mythical Buddhist cosmos.

3. World maps representing Chinese thought. These maps were copies of Chinese maps showing China prominently in the center with other countries arranged around it.

4. World maps in which Japan (specifically, Kyoto) is the center of the world. Ayusawa says that they were much more scientific than the two previous categories and were a reaction against Chinese and Buddhist concepts placing China and India at the center of the world.

5. Legendary world maps. These included illustrations showing grotesque and mysterious figures and monsters. According to Ayusawa, they demonstrated "the ignorance of the Japanese during the period of seclusion."

Ayusawa notes that the Japanese world maps produced during this time used various projections: Ortelius's egg-shaped maps, hemispheric maps showing the world projected as eastern and western hemispheres, maps using Mercator's projection, and maps not based on any known system. Some world maps were copied from manuscripts. Others were printed first from woodblocks, but from the end of the eighteenth century, beginning with the *Chikyūzu* (World Map) of Shiba Kōkan, copper plates were also used. Many of the maps had explanatory texts concerning astronomy as well as geography.

Because knowledge of the outside world gained through the so-called Dutch studies was very inadequately propagated, popular world maps produced as late as the 1830s and 1840s depicted America and Africa in shapes reminiscent of sixteenth-century European maps, and Australia was often not shown at all. The results of Captain Cook's voyages were thus unknown to the ordinary educated Japanese half a century or more after they were disseminated in the West.

The development of Japanese cities and the increase in the number of travelers created a demand for city maps (*toshizu*), local maps (*chihōzu*), and route maps (*dōchū-zu*). Many of these have survived, especially from the early nineteenth century (Pl. 52), but some earlier ones have also been preserved. The British Library, to whom the famous collection of books and manuscripts made in the late seventeenth century by Engelbert Kaempfer came through Sir Hans Sloane, has a fine seventeenth-century map of Nagasaki (Pl. 50) which is particularly attractive. Understandably, the most popular maps were those of Edo (Pl. 54), but maps of Kyoto (Pl. 56) and Osaka are relatively easy to find. Maps of Nagasaki, Kamakura (Pl. 57), and of places such as Nikkō and other towns can also be found. In later years detailed maps of sections of cities were produced, especially of Edo (Pl. 58.)

One feature of Japanese maps in this period was that they were normally folded into a small size and when opened were generally looked at while sitting on the floor. The directions and the writing were thus meant to be read from four different directions. As a result, there is sometimes no obvious top and bottom, although gradually north began, in European fashion, to be regarded as being at the top.

Another noteworthy phenomenon was the Japanese liking for panoramic maps in which mountains, castles, towns, forests, and other features were shown in pictorial form as if seen from the air. The vogue for panoramic maps and the popularity of the journey from Edo to Kyoto and Osaka led such prominent artists as Hokusai to produce bird's-eye maps, especially of the Tōkaidō route including, naturally, views of Mount Fuji (Pls. 59,60,61). Some of these maps are among the most artistic of all Japanese maps, even if from a cartographic point of view they have distinct drawbacks and are highly inaccurate.

Thus, by the middle of the nineteenth century Japan had a highly developed mapmaking industry, and maps of various kinds were in much demand. The best, such as those of Inō Tadataka, were very good, while the more popular maps were attractive, if inaccurate.

European Maps of Japan During the Years of Seclusion

During the Tokugawa period, European maps of Japan improved slowly, but despite a number of voyages of exploration in the seventeenth century, progress was uneven. In the latter part of the seventeenth century and early eighteenth century there was a distinct regression. This is not surprising when the seclusion policy of the Tokugawa shogunate is taken into account. The export of maps was banned, although some undoubtedly were sent abroad during Japan's so-called Christian century. Richard Cocks, the Head of the British factory in Hirado, in a letter of November 30, 1613, reported that William Adams had drawn out a plot of Japan and sent it to the British East India Company by the hand of Captain Saris on the Clove. Unfortunately it has not survived.

Strenuous efforts were later made to prevent any light from seeping to the outside world through the tiny, shuttered window that was Deshima, the Dutch outpost off Nagasaki. But while many of the Dutch factors were dull and ill-educated men, intent only on serving out their time and earning some easy money, the Dutch also had some highly intelligent and observant servants. Three of these were outstanding: Engelbert Kaempfer (1651–1716), Carl Peter Thunberg (1743–1822), who was in Japan from 1775 to 1776, and Philip Franz von Siebold (1796–1866). All were doctors to the mission. Kaempfer and Siebold were of German origin. Thunberg was a Swede. All were scientifically trained and their curiosity was insatiable. Two of them, Kaempfer and Siebold, were particularly interested in maps and managed to smuggle out some Japanese maps. Unfortunately those brought out by Kaempfer were still very inaccurate and much influenced by the Gyōgi tradition, but the maps which Siebold saw, and in some cases managed to copy, were far and away better than most of the current European maps of Japan. Nagasaki thus became an important if intermittent and unreliable source of information for the European cartographers during these 250 years.

Of even greater importance as far as the Japanese coastline is concerned were the voyages of exploration which were undertaken first by the Dutch in the seventeenth century and then by Russians, French, and British mariners in the eighteenth and early nineteenth centuries. Many of these voyages were of particular importance in relation to the exploration of Hokkaido and the northern islands discussed later. A brief account must, however, be given here of a few of the main voyages which ensured that by 1806 only the Inland Sea, the northwest coast of Honshu, and the north coast of Hokkaido remained unsurveyed by Europeans.

The first important Dutch expedition was sent out in 1639 by the governor-general of the Dutch East Indies, Antonio van Diemen (it will be recalled that an early name for Australia was Van Diemen's land). His attention had been drawn in 1635 by a Dutch merchant named Versteegen to the alleged existence of gold and silver mines in the North Pacific east of Japan. The expedition's task was to discover these islands. Mathys Quast was appointed Commander of the expedition and he hoisted his flag on the Dutch ship Engel. He was accompanied by Abel Janszoon Tasman (after whom Tasmania was named) in command of the Gracht. Their instructions provided that if they could not find the islands they were to go around Japan and explore the coasts of Tartary, China, and Korea. Quast, in fact, only touched the main Japanese islands at three points. His major discovery was the Bonin Islands, although these had been visited earlier by Spanish and Portuguese mariners, among them Bernardo de la Torre, Captain of the galleon of the expedition of Ruy Lopez de Villalobos in 1543.

In 1643 the Dutch sent Martin Gerritsz Vries in command of the Bresken to follow up on Quast and Tasman. When he set out, Vries was given various papers, including the atlases of Willem and Johann Blaeu (1571–1638 and 1596–1673), the *Itinerario* of Linschóten (published in 1599), and "two sketch maps of the gold islands as the same is depicted in the Japanese Beobys," (*byōbu*, or folding screen). This was one of the most important voyages of discovery ever undertaken in relation to Japan. Vries clarified almost all of that part of the main island which Western explorers had not yet visited, but as his survey of the northern territories was intermittent, his report was the cause of a number of subsequent errors.

The Russians began to explore to the north of Japan as early as the mid-seventeenth century, but while their voyages were of great significance in relation to Hokkaido and the Kuriles, they contributed little to the knowledge of the other islands.

After Vries, little significant exploration of the coasts of the main islands occurred until the latter part of the eighteenth century. After the murder of Captain Cook, two of his captains, Gore and King, sailed along the east coast of Japan, but the general map of Captain Cook's voyages was inaccurate in its depiction of this coast. Moreover, Tōhoku was shown as being wider than it actually is.

The French mariner La Pérouse (Jean François de Galaup, Comte de la Pérouse, born 1741, died by shipwreck in 1788; Pl. 62) traveled in 1787 to the southwest coast of Formosa, to the Tsushima straits, to the Japanese coast around the Nōtō Peninsula, as well as to the province of Amur in Siberia, the west coast of Sakhalin, and the Southern Kurile Islands. The British mariner William Robert Broughton, in 1797, traveled almost completely around Formosa, surveyed the Ryukyu Islands, the south coast of Kyushu, the coast of Honshu from the Kii Peninsula as far as the Tsugaru Straits, as well as areas to the north.* In 1805, the Russian mariner Adam Johann von Krusenstern (1770–1846; he published an atlas of the Pacific in St. Petersburg

*One of Captain Broughton's two ships, HMS Providence, of four hundred tons and sixteen guns, foundered on a hidden reef off Miyakojima in the Ryukyus in May 1797. He and his 115 men were well received and eventually got away on the second ship, a schooner. After visiting Macao and putting most of his men on another ship, he continued his survey, visiting Naha in Okinawa in July. Broughton's report impressed the Admiralty, and a full survey of the currents, reefs, and shoals throughout the Ryukyu Islands was proposed; but mainly because of the preoccupations of the Napoleonic wars, this had to wait until 1816. In that year

in two sections, the first in 1826–27, the second in 1837–38) practically completed the task, traveling not only around much of the northern territories, but also the west coast of Honshu as far as Akita, the Tsushima Straits, and most of Kyushu. These latter surveys were relatively accurate and showed only slight misreadings of longitude and latitude as compared with admiralty charts of 1909.

The most significant of the seventeenth-century European maps of Japan was that by Father Martini (1614–61; Pl. 63), which appeared in the 1655 *Atlas Sinensis* of John Blaeu, although the map was drawn in 1649. This was one of the first European maps of Japan on which the east coast of Honshu from the Bōsō Peninsula northward was drawn in accordance with de Vries's discoveries. It was also generally more accurate than any other European maps of the seventeenth century and indeed than most other European maps before the surveys of the late eighteenth century brought a new accuracy to the depiction of the Japanese coastline. Father Martino Martini, a Jesuit, went to China as a young man and eventually became the superior at Hangzhou. His *Imperii Sinarum Nova Descriptio*, which shows the interrelationship between China, Korea, and Japan, appeared in 1650. In 1651 he left for Rome, taking three years on an eventful journey home. After a short stay in Europe he returned to Hangzhou, where he remained until he died. There is no evidence that Martini ever visited Japan; indeed, this seems most unlikely in view of the Japanese persecution of Christians, but he surely must have had access to the history of Japan, *This Island of Japon*, by the Portuguese Jesuit João Rodrigues (1561?–1633). Rodrigues's life and works have been ably and fully described by Michael Cooper in his book *Rodrigues the Interpreter*. But Rodrigues's account of Japanese geography was not very scientific. Martini's map was the basis for a number of later maps, including that of the

Captain Basil Hall in HMS Lyra and Captain Sir Murray Maxwell in HMS Alceste spent some six weeks in the area of Okinawa and carried out the long-awaited survey. Captain Hall and Dr. McLeod, the surgeon on the Alceste, published accounts of their experiences praising the warm welcome accorded them by the Okinawans despite the Japanese ban on foreign intercourse, which was only very partially enforced in the Ryukyu Islands. British ships made fairly frequent visits to Okinawa in the years leading up to the opening of Japan.

English cartographer Robert Morden in 1680. This map, entitled *Japonae ac Terrae Iessonis Novissima Descriptio*, shows Hokkaido connected to Korea (Pl. 85).

Martini's map, significant though it is, was not the only new European map to supercede that of Teixeira. Father Antonio Francisco Cardim (ca. 1595–1659 or 1596–1649) produced a map of Japan (Pl. 64) which was published in Rome in 1646. This is said to have been compiled some years earlier. Cardim became procurator general of the Jesuits in Japan but never actually got to Japan. He, too, almost certainly had access to Rodrigues's history as well as to the accounts of Ignacio Moreira. Cardim's was the first European map to show all the sixty-six provinces. His map was very similar to that of Bernardino Ginnaro, whose work, *Saverio Orientale*, appeared in 1641.

This latter map was the basis for the *Carta Piu Moderna* by Robert Dudley. Sir Robert Dudley, styled Duke of Northumberland in the Holy Roman Empire, was born in about 1574. In 1594 he was the first Englishman to go 250 miles up the Orinoco River, the third longest river in South America. He seems to have come into the service of the Grand Duke of Tuscany in about 1606 and to have lived for at least thirty years in Florence and Leghorn (Livorno). Dudley's manuscript maps, which have been preserved in the Staatsbibliothek in Munich, are nautical charts depicting primarily coastlines. They were prepared in the years leading up to 1636. Versions of these maps were published in Dudley's atlas, *Arcano del Mare*, in Florence in 1646–47. A second, revised, and enlarged edition was also published in 1661 in Florence. J.F. Schütte, who has done a careful study of these maps, has commented that his representation of Japan "is without question original and based on his own studies, but not on firsthand knowledge of the country." Indeed not, or he would not have made so many extraordinary errors. Schütte suggests that among Dudley's sources was a Gyōgi-type map with south at the top and north at the bottom. This might, for instance, account for the fact that in one of his maps the Meaco River flows north from Meaco (Miyako, or Kyoto), and where the river joins the sea to the east lies the province of Musashi with the city of Yedo (Edo) at its mouth.

In the *Asia carta di ciasete piu moderna* (Pl. 65), published in the second edition of 1661, Meaco is shown to the east of a large lagoon running in from the Inland Sea. Another map of Japan, *Carta Particolare della Grande Isola de 'Giapone è di Iezo con il Regno di Corai et altre Isole in torno* (Pl. 66), shows the Ōmi River (Ōmi is the name of the province which now forms Shiga Prefecture and is often used to describe the area around Lake Biwa) running north. Meaco appears to be on a small lake with a river emerging in the sea about two-thirds of the way down a most inaccurate depiction of the Kii Peninsula. "Surunga" (Suruga, the present Shizuoka) is shown on the north coast of Honshu, not the south, as it should be. The River Negata (presumably a reference to Niigata) is shown on the east coast (not the west coast, as it should be) of a truncated and much-compressed Tōhoku. Most of the place names are diffi-cult if not impossible to identify.

Another interesting map of this period was that produced by Father Philippe Briet (1601–68; Pl. 67). This was published by Mariette in Paris in 1650. Father Briet was a Jesuit from Abbeville. While his depiction of the shape of Japan showed some improvement over that of Teixeira, his errors were as great as those of Dudley. Most astonishing, in view of the fact that of all the Japanese islands the best known to the Europeans was the southern island, is his depiction of Kyushu as a series of islands divided by canals or rivers. He also shows Lake Biwa as an inlet of Osaka Bay. He clearly never went to Japan and his research was faulty. Rodrigues was sarcastic about people who drew maps of Japan but had never visited the country.* In the case of seventeenth-century geographers this was rather unfair as most of them had no pos-sibility of getting to Japan or, if they did, of finding out much about Japanese geo-graphy.

In the second half of the seventeenth century, a number of other interesting if still very inaccurate maps of Japan were published in Europe. Nicolas Sanson

*Rodrigues in 1616 wrote: "Everything in the [European] maps at present in circulation is full of errors and names are scattered about at will and without any accuracy." In 1627, in another letter, he said: "And new men will come who fill books with make-believe just like the other books dealing with these regions and Japan which they wrote while in Europe. If an angel were to come and clean up these false books, we'd have an abundance of clean paper for some years."

(1600–67) was born in Abbeville, and his map of Japan, which appeared in *L'Asie,* Paris, 1652, under the title *Description Des Isles de Iapon en Sept Principales Parties,* followed fairly closely that of Father Briet, his fellow countryman, although his depiction of Kyushu was more realistic. Sanson declared that his sources were Father Cardim and the Dutch geographer Bernhard Varen (Varennus in Latin), whose *Descriptio Regni Japoniae* first appeared in 1649. A later issue by his family after his death in 1683, *Les Isles du Iapon* (Pl. 68), was not much better.

Jan Jansson (1588–1664), who married Hondius's daughter, included a "new and accurate" map of Japan (Pl. 70) and the land of Ezo with the adjacent islands in his *Nieuwen Atlas,* which appeared in Amsterdam in 1659. For the main islands Jansson took Teixeira's map as his model (see p. 25), but he also took account of the chart compiled by Vries of his voyage of 1643. Inaccuracies in Honshu include the depiction of the Yodogawa as rising in Lake Biwa and emerging in the sea some way south of Osaka, whereas it flows around Osaka. He also omits the Nōtō Peninsula altogether.

More interesting is the *Perfeckte Kaert vande gelegentheydt des Landts van Iapan* by François Caron (1600–73; Pl. 69). Although this was drawn probably as early as 1636, it was published in The Hague only in 1661. Caron spent over twenty-two years in Japan. He obtained a good working knowledge of Japanese, visited Edo on numerous occasions, and became head of the Dutch factory in Japan at a crucial time, 1639. Professor Boxer argues that if it had not been for Caron, the Dutch as well as the Portuguese might have been expelled from Japan in the first half of the seventeenth century. Caron concluded his career in the service of the French after some checkered dealings with the Dutch East India Company. He died at sea. Together with Joost Schooten he wrote *A True Description of the Mighty Kingdoms of Japan and Siam.* This English edition was published in London in 1663. Caron's map is remarkable for the fact that it shows Japan connected by a strip of land to Jesso (Ezo, or Hokkaido), which is in turn shown as being joined to Tartary.

An amusing if inaccurate seventeenth-century map is that by Jean-Baptiste Tavernier (1605–89) which appeared in Paris in 1679 under the title *Carte des Isles du Iapon Esquelles est remarqué la Route tant par Mer que par Terre que Tiennent les Hollandois pour se transporter de la Ville de Nangasaqui a Iedo demeure du Roy de ces mesmes Isles* (Pl. 71). The map, which is on a fairly large scale, contains comments about the nature of the country. For instance, Ocasaqui (Okazaki, near Nagoya) is said to have the most beautiful women—"C'est ou sont les plus belles femmes du pays." Lake Biwa is said to be where one can catch "quantité de saumons." Mount Fuji is described as "Fusino-omma, montagne toujours couverte de neige." An island, which could be Tsushima, off the coast of Kyushu is described as "l'Isle ou on envoie la jeunesse, qui ne veut rien valoir et ou on les fait travailler par force, jusqu' a ce que leur proches les en retire" (the island where worthless youths are sent and made to work until their relations remove them)! Tavernier marked three places where there were alleged to be silver mines. Unfortunately the map is very inaccurate. Matsushima is, for instance, shown as a long north-south island off a part of Honshu called Ochior (Ōshū). Kyushu and Shikoku are shown as much smaller than in other seventeenth-century maps and than they really are. Jean Gaspar Scheuchzer, in his introduction to Kaempfer's *History of Japan*, says of Tavernier: "That author, himself scarce able to read or write and obliged to borrow the pen of another man to write the account of his travels, was too superficial in his description even of those countries where he hath been and too apt, not only to take things upon trust at first hand, but afterwards also to confide too much to his memory, to be anyways depended on."

Another source of information about Japan, even if inaccurate and imaginative rather than factual and realistic, was the book of Arnoldus Montanus, published in 1699 in Dutch in Amsterdam. An English edition by John Ogilby appeared in 1670. This contained two route maps, covering the two parts of the author's journey, entitled *De Land Reyse van Osacca tot Iedo* and *De Water Reyse van Nangasacqui tot Osacca*. These may well have been based on Japanese route maps. But Montanus had only a hazy if poetic idea of Japanese geography. He wrote: "The Empire or Island of Japan, if it be an Isle, is not only one, but many; which evidently appears by those parts that border on the Sea, where the coast discontinued with many In-lets, stands like a broke wall, and the several falls of fresh water Brooks and Rivulets, descending from the upper grounds, with their mixt interweavings,

47

both from Sea and Land, make a numerous crowd of petty Isles; from which watery redundancy, arise cloudy exhalations, that cause variety of stirring weather." Montanus also included engravings of Osaka, Edo, and Miyako which can only be described as based on imagination (Pls. 72, 73). Scheuchzer was as scathing about Montanus as he was of Tavernier: "This work doth by no means answer neither the expense bestowed on the impression, nor the promises made in the very title page, nor doth it deserve the favourable reception it hath met with. It is full of large degressions. . . ."

Mention must also be made of another seventeenth-century map, namely that published by the Venetian cartographer Vincenzo Maria Coronelli in 1692 under the title *Isola del Giapone e Peninsola di Corea* (Pl. 75). Coronelli used Dutch mariners' charts as well as Jesuit sources. Honshu is depicted on the lines adopted by Martini, but mountain ranges are delineated pictorially. The Gulf of Tosa in Shikoku is not shown. In the Sea of Japan a somewhat Italianate vessel with a large bank of twenty oars is afloat. It is described as being used on the route from Nagasaki to Osaka, a distance which it is said to travel in twelve days.

The most important influence on European maps of Japan during the early years of the eighteenth century was that of Engelbert Kaempfer. Kaempfer was born in Westphalia in 1651. After studying at various places in North Germany and in Poland, he applied himself to the study of natural sciences at Königsberg in Russia and at Upsla in Sweden. He traveled in Russia and Persia, eventually reaching Batavia (now Jakarta) in the Dutch East Indies in 1689. In May 1690 he left Batavia for Japan, having been appointed physician to the embassy which the Dutch East India Company sent once a year to the shogun's court in Edo. He stayed in Japan until November 1692, returning to Europe in 1693. He died in 1716. His two-volume *History of Japan* translated into English by Scheuchzer and first published in 1727 is not only a fascinating account of his stay in Japan but also a detailed study of the country and its institutions (insofar as he was allowed to observe them) as well as the flora and fauna of the country. His account of the embassy to Edo during which he and his colleagues were forced to dance and perform for the amusement of the shogun is particularly memorable. Kaempfer's meticulous attention to detail and his able draftsmanship can be seen in the large number of illustrations contained in his work. Chapter 5 of Book 1 of Kaempfer's *History* was, according to Scheuchzer, Kaempfer's editor, based on the *Sitzi Jossu* [sic], *A Geographical Description of the Empire of Japan*. This consists of a brief account of the main areas of Japan divided into the traditional *dō*, or routes, such as the Tōkaidō, San'yōdō, and several others.

One of the main points of interest in the map included in Kaempfer's *History* (Pl. 76) is that the names of the provinces are not only given in romanized versions as on previous maps but also in Chinese characters. These are slightly odd in some respects, suggesting that they were copied by someone who was not a native of Japan or China. Cartographically, it was a retrogression from Martini's map and other European maps of the latter seventeenth century. Kaempfer's model may have been his copy of an Ishikawa Ryūsen map. Tōhoku remains foreshortened, but at least in the Kaempfer-Scheuchzer map it does turn northward.

Adrien Reland's map of 1715 (Pl. 77) was first published in French in Amsterdam by the Ottens brothers and in Latin in Utrecht. Adrien Reland (1678–1718) was a Dutch orientalist at the University of Utrecht, a scholar rather than a traveler. Reland, in a long marginal note on the inset map of Nagasaki, stated that his map was based on a manuscript sketch by one of his countrymen, who also indicated all the details of the coastline of southwest Japan from Hirado to Nagasaki. His depiction of the feudal provinces is said to have been based on a Japanese map in the library of one Benjamin Dutry, a former director of the Dutch East India Company. Like Kaempfer, he gave the characters for the provinces, the shapes of the characters suggesting a similar source. Tōhoku appears to the east of Edo.

Henry Abraham Chatelain (1684–1743) was a French cartographer. His map published in 1719 was basically a copy of Reland's, although it was decorated in a different way. Another of his maps is shown in Plate 74. The map of Japan by Mattheus Seutter (1678–1757; Pl. 78), published in Augsburg in 1745, was also essentially a copy of the Reland-Chatelain map and was equally highly decorated.

There are several other noteworthy eighteenth-century European maps of Japan.

Pieter van der Aa (1659–1733) published a small map of Japan at Leyden in Holland in 1707. This map (Pl. 79)is interesting for the charming vignette in the cartouche of William Adams at the court of the shogun. The map is, however, a throwback to the early seventeenth century, as it shows Korea once again as an island. It looks indeed like a copy of Sanson's map of 1652. Herman Moll (1688–1745), a Dutch cartographer who worked in England, published another small map of Japan in London in 1712. This showed the results of Vries's survey, but is otherwise not noteworthy.

The map *Nieuwe Kaart van't Keizerryk Japan* by Isaac Tirion (died 1761; Pl. 80) was first published in Amsterdam in 1735. It showed the names of the provinces as transliterated by the Dutch. The outline of Japan is generally inaccurate, but it does show the main areas of Japan such as the Hokuriku and the Sanin districts.

The French cartographer Jacques Nicholas Bellin (1703–72) produced various maps of Japan. His first was published in 1735, with others in 1746, 1752, and 1763. He also produced a map of Nagasaki in 1763, the *Plan du Port et de la Ville de Nangasaki* (Pl. 51), which Campbell identifies as a "close copy" of a J. van Schley map dated 1752. Bellin's maps remained very inaccurate. Even the 1763 version shows Kyushu slanted to the east with Nagasaki and the nearby peninsula almost parallel with southern Kyushu. Shikoku is almost square, except for a deep inlet on the north side. The Oki Islands are exaggerated and the Izumo area of what is now Shimane Prefecture is grossly distorted, as is the Noto Peninsula, while Tohoku remains foreshortened. Nevertheless, Bellin's maps influenced other cartographers. Emanuel Bowen (died 1767) published in London in 1747 *A New and Accurate Map of the Empire of Japan* (Pl. 81), which he admitted was a copy of Bellin's.

George Louis Lerouge, who was active between 1741 and 1779, published a map of Japan (Pl. 82) in Paris in 1748. This exaggerated the size of Korea in relation to Japan, but Tōhoku was more accurately drawn than in many previous maps. Another Paris map, that of Robert de Vaugondy (1688–1766), which was published in 1749 and 1750, was much on the lines of Bellin's map. Antonio Zatta (1757–97) published in Venice in 1785 a map of the Japanese Empire which continued to show most of the inaccuracies of earlier eighteenth-century maps. The map of the Japanese Empire published in London in 1790 by Robert Sayer, a British map seller who flourished between 1780 and 1810, was similar to that of Robert de Vaugondy. Thus the eighteenth century ended without any accurate Western maps of Japan. These had to wait the result of the surveys of La Pérouse, Broughton, and Krusenstern, as well as the result of Siebold's studies.

Philip Franz von Siebold was born in Würzburg in 1796. After studying medicine, he became in 1822 a surgeon major in the employ of the Dutch East India Company. He arrived in Nagasaki in August 1823 as doctor to the Dutch factory, and in 1826 accompanied the Dutch mission to Edo. He was particularly interested in natural sciences and, like his predecessors Kaempfer and Thunberg, was extremely conscientious, thorough, and persistent. During the journey to Edo he made secret measurements of heights and distances and even managed a hydrographic survey of the straits of Shimonoseki. When some of the Japanese officials accompanying the Dutch mission became suspicious of his surveying, he explained that his observations were essential for the regulation of the mission's clocks. His measurement of the height of Mount Fuji was later regarded, at his trial for sedition, as a particularly grave offence. In fact it proved an especially difficult task for him as he had to make his own height barometer. At Edo he managed to gain access to the shogun's library, where he found Japanese maps of the territories to the north of Honshu. He got hold of works by Japanese travelers and geographers, including a map by Mogami Tokunai (1755–1836), a diary by Mamiya Rinzō, and a work by Takahashi Kageyasu, then astronomer to the shogun's court.

Siebold recorded in his diary on the 16th of December, 1825, that Joshio Tsujiro, underinterpreter at the Dutch factory on Deshima in Nagasaki, who was as usual helping with translations from Japanese works (on this occasion some handwritten information by Mogami Tokunai about Ezo and his travels), was very ill at ease and seemed in a bad humor. Siebold thought that this mood might be due to the fact that he had not yet carried out his promise to give the interpreter his pocket chronometer. But Tsujiro eventually revealed that Siebold's interest in Japanese maps had been betrayed to the authorities. He, Tsujiro, had been arrested and released only when he had given an undertaking to hand over to the authorities the maps which had been brought by Siebold from Edo. In order to gain time, they decided that Tsujiro would hand over to the authorities those maps of which Siebold had duplicate copies and would produce the following day the large map which Siebold had of Hokkaido and Sakhalin, to which the authorities attached particular importance and which had been obtained from the astronomer Takahashi. Siebold then sat up all night making a copy of the map and a translation of the text. As Siebold had been warned that his effects would be searched, he handed this copy to Maylan, the head of the Dutch factory, to keep for him and to demonstrate that his behavior had been justified by his geographical discoveries. Siebold's pupils and friends were arrested, and Siebold, who was left to his fate by the Dutch, was interrogated and forbidden to leave, while his effects were searched and some items were confiscated. At first the Japanese suspected a plot to hand over the country to a foreign power, and Deshima itself was searched and placed under even stricter guard. In June 1829 some of Siebold's servants were released, but many of his friends spent years in prison and Takahashi died there. Others found refuge with daimyo such as those of Satsuma and Awajima, who were increasingly opposed to the Tokugawa shogunate. Siebold was finally allowed to leave Japan on January 2, 1830.*

Although the most important items in his collection were withheld, Siebold retained enough to enable him, with his excellent memory, to produce more accurate Western maps of Japan than any prepared earlier. One of these appeared under the title *Japanisches Reich* in 1840 (Pl. 83) and as *Nippon* in 1852. This was apparently later used as the basis for admiralty charts, although it contains some errors probably due to the speed at which Siebold had had to copy Japanese originals, including, probably, maps by Inō Tadataka. Indeed, it has been argued that Siebold's map is little more than an inaccu-

*Siebold returned to Nagasaki in 1859 after the reopening of Japan and resumed his studies. He was summoned by the shogunate to Edo in 1861, but soon returned to Java in the hope that he would be nominated to a high diplomatic post in Japan by the Dutch. Responsibility for relations with Japan had, however, by then passed from the administration of the Dutch East Indies to the Foreign Ministry at The Hague, and Siebold's hopes were disappointed. He died, embittered, in Munich on October 18, 1866.

rate copy of Inō's. Siebold's maps represented a major step forward in the cartography of Japan, even though they still contained some minor errors. By now the outline of the Japanese coastline was pretty accurately known in the West, and the maps produced in the early part of the nineteenth century can no longer be considered as antiques, however interesting they may be from a historical point of view.

The collector of nineteenth-century maps is likely to find copies of John Tallis's map of Japan (Pl. 90), which appeared in his *Illustrated Atlas of the World*. The outline is reasonably accurate, but the decoration owes a good deal to Montanus, and the ship depicted on the map is a copy of that on Coronelli's map. The map at the beginning of Sir Rutherford Alcock's *The Capital of the Tycoon*, 1863, said to be based on a Japanese map, is considerably less accurate than that of Tallis.

The Northern Islands: Japanese and European
Exploration and Early Maps of the Area

The northern islands were almost unknown, even to the Japanese, until about the sixteenth century, and were not properly explored until the end of the eighteenth century. It seems therefore appropriate to consider separately Japanese and Western knowledge of the northern islands and how this was reflected in early maps.

Japanese and European maps of Japan make no mention of Ezo, the modern Hokkaido, until about the end of the sixteenth century, unless the territory in Gyōgi-type maps named Gandō (or Kari no Michi) is Ezo—which is hardly certain. Even when Ezo was mentioned, the depiction of the territory was hazy and inaccurate. Indeed, the Japanese were not even clear that it was an island, and Europeans had even vaguer conceptions. Many thought Ezo was part of the North Asian mainland.

The first Japanese reference to Ezo has been traced to the reign of Empress Saimei (ca. 655–61), when one Abe no Hirafu was sent to Watarishima to subdue the native Ainus. Before the Nara period (710–82), all of northeastern Japan including Tōhoku was called Koshi, and its inhabitants were called Koshibito by the Japanese. (Koshibito literally means "people from over the other side.") Koshi in due course was corrupted to Kui or Kai. When Chinese characters were imported from Asia, characters meaning "eastern barbarian people" were used for Kai and the pronunciation of Ezo or Yezo was adopted.

Northern Honshu, or Tōhoku, came under Japanese rule only in the middle of the eleventh century, and the Abe family, which took control of the area, had only

54

a very shadowy connection with the territory to the north of Honshu. It was not in fact until the twelfth century that scattered Japanese settlements were founded on the Ōshima Peninsula of Ezo by refugees from the wars between the Minamoto and the Taira. In the Kamakura period (1185–1333) there was a reference to Eso no Chishima, the Ainu islands. In the fourteenth century, a fief under the Andō family was established, but they appear to have exercised little real control of the territory. However, in about 1442 Takeda Nobuhiro, who adopted the name of Kakizaki, established a firmer grip on at least the southern part of the area. The Takeda family acted largely independently from such central regimes as existed in Japan during the Ashikaga period. Eventually they accepted the suzerainty of Toyotomi Hideyoshi, when they adopted the name of Matsumae. Matsumae was also the castle town and became for some time synonymous with Ezo.

The *Shūgaishō* which appeared at the beginning of the seventeenth century, contained the first printed Japanese map to refer to Ezo, under the name Ezochi, although Ezo was mentioned in manuscript maps such as the Tōshōdai-ji map and in Korean maps of 1402 and 1471. The name Matsumae first appeared in records at the time of Ashikaga Takauji (1305–58). A ten-day journey from east to west passed through Matsumae during the Tembun era (1532–54), and a map was apparently drawn of this journey and presented to Toyotomi Hideyoshi in 1594, but has not survived. A "complete" map of Ezo was also reported to have been presented to Tokugawa Ieyasu in 1599, but this too has disappeared. Another early expedition at the time of Toyotomi Hideyoshi is said to have spent two years unsuccessfully trying to cross Ezo from north to south.

In view of Japanese ignorance and general lack of interest in Ezo up to that time, it is hardly surprising that the first Western maps of Japan generally omitted any mention of Ezo, although a reference to Ezo was contained in a letter written on December 26, 1548, by Father Nicholo Lancilotto from the Jesuit house in Cochin, a region of Vietnam. On the basis of information from a Japanese called Yajiro, he described the inhabitants of "Gsoo" to the northeast of Japan as being "white with long whiskers; they are tall and fight fearlessly, one against a hundred, like the

Germans." Another early reference to Ezo was contained in a letter from Father Luis Frois dated at Kyoto, February 20, 1565; he spoke of a spacious land of wild people and large bears. William Adams, too, had heard of Ezo and sent home to the East India Company in 1613 a map showing part of "Yedzo," but the map has not survived.

The first European to visit Ezo was almost certainly Girolamo (or Jeronimo) de Angelis, a Jesuit priest, who probably went there in 1618 and again in 1621. Father Diego Carvalho also seems to have visited the island in 1620. De Angelis, in his report, discussed the arguments for and against Ezo being an island; he concluded that it was one and appended a manuscript map (Pl. 84). De Angelis showed Ezo as having a coastline near to Korea and with only a narrow strait between the north of Ezo and Tartary. The size of Ezo was thus grossly exaggerated, but his outline of Tōhoku, particularly his depiction of the northward slope, was an improvement on other contemporary maps.

The Europeans continued for over a century to debate the question of whether Ezo was an island or not. The mapmakers generally avoided the issue in their maps of Japan by referring to Ezo simply as a territory or land and frequently, as in the maps by Briet (1650), and Martini (1655), by showing only the most southerly tip. Briet showed the Tsugaru Straits as being narrow while Martini drew a large stretch of sea between Honshu and Ezo. Caron (1661) showed Honshu and Ezo connected by an isthmus: "The countrey of Japan is supposed to bee an Island, though there bee no certainty of it, this vast territorie not beeing yet wholly discovered to the inhabitants themselves. I have often enquired and been informed that Travellers have come from the Province of Quanto [Kanto, or the area round Edo] wherein the Imperial Citie and Palace of Iedo are situated 27 daies North-East wards, before they could reach the utmost point of the land of Sungaer [Tsugaru], bordering upon the Sea; being come thither they passed over an Istmus of thirty-three English miles broad, leading into the Countrey of Iezzo [Ezo] abounding in skins and furrs of price. This territorie is very great, mountainous but little inhabited. The Iappaners attempted its discovery severall times but in vaine, for though they entered to and fro, far into the Countrey, yet they could never find its end, nor any certainty concerning it, their provisions ordinarily failing them, which enforced their fruitless returnes. The discoverers reports of these were soe imperfect that his Majestic despaired of any further satisfaction, the countrey being presented as desolate and unpassable, though in some places inhabited with a people all over hairy (wearing their beards long, like the Chinese) and brutish, though otherwise well shaped. To consider whether this country be an island or no, wee may observe that the passage betweene Sungaer and Iezzo is no running water but an inlet or long Istmus of the Sea itselfe, 120 English Miles long, extending itselfe between Iezzo and Iapan, where it bounds upon vast mountaines and deserts, about the Province of Ochio [Ōshū], so that, that way being wholly unpassable by land, travellers are forced to ferry over the aforesaid Istmus from Sungaer to Iezzo, in Barkes and such shipping as they have.'' Caron's view of Ezo was adopted by Montanus.

Vries, however, had sailed along the east coast of Ezo in 1643, passed between the two most southerly islands in the Kurile chain, which he named Statenland (Kunashiri) and Compagniesland (Etorofu), and reached the southern end of Sakhalin Island (called Karafuto by the Japanese) although he missed the strait to the south of it. On three important points he got the positions wrong, namely, over the connection between Kunashiri and Ezo, the absence of a strait between this and Sakhalin, and the hypothesis that the territory which he named Compagniesland was America. These mistakes were not at first noticed and led for a long time to an almost totally inaccurate picture of Ezo appearing in Western maps. Jansson, who largely based his map on Vries's survey, left too wide a gap between Honshu and Ezo on the lines of Martini's map. He then shows the Landt Van Eso coming down from the north in a bow turning eastwards with Staten Eylant and then a huge Compagniesland. Jansson also continued the error of showing Korea as an island.

Further confusion arose as a result of a voyage by a Portuguese merchant João de Gama of Macao who, while sailing from China to Mexico via the northern route, seems to have had a glimpse of the Kuriles. His findings were incorporated in a map drawn by João Teixeira in 1649 which was redrawn in the light of Vries's discoveries and published by Melchisedech Thevenot (1620–92) in 1664. In this map the northern shore of Ezo was shown by a dotted line. It also showed a territory called Gamaland, which may be Etorofu or Vries's Compagniesland.

In the light of all this contradictory evidence, Western geographers not only continued to have doubts about whether Ezo was an island but even whether it was or was not connected to Honshu. The French cartographer, Guillaume Delisle (1675–1726), stated on his map of 1705 (Pl. 86) that it was not known whether Ezo was connected with Honshu or not. Another map of the same period (Pl. 88) shows them nearly touching. In a letter of 1715, he declared that the position could not be clarified as no maps by Japanese cartographers existed in Europe. In this he was, of course, wrong.

Even Kaempfer, despite all his conscientious efforts, was unable to clarify the issues, because Japanese accounts were contradictory. Scheuchzer, in his introduction to Kaempfer's *History*, wrote: "Some maps place between Japan [Honshu] and Jesogashima [Ezo] another small island called Matsumai." He added: "I must own, that these maps, for accuracy and preciseness, fall far short of our European ones, the Eastern geographers being not skilled enough in Mathematicks and astronomy for that." Kaempfer himself refers to Matsumai as a neighboring island belonging to Ōshū, and adds that "it is said to be as large as the Island Kiusiu [Kyushu]." "As to its figure, I could not gather anything positive, neither from the accounts I had from the Japanese, nor from the Maps, I met with in the Country, they differing much from each other. Some represent it very near round, others make it of a very irregular figure, with large Promontories, Gulphs and Bays, the Sea running in several places so far up into the country that one might be easily induc'd to believe it compos'd of several different Islands." He also wrote of the "Continent of Okujeso" —presumably Kamchatka. He found that the Japanese knew very little of this area: "I was little the better for consulting the Japanese Maps of those Seas." In these circumstances it is not surprising that Bellin's and Tirion's maps of Japan of 1735 make Matsumai into a small island.

Meanwhile Japanese interest in Ezo and the territories to the north gradually increased, not least to counter growing Russian attention in the area. In 1633 the daimyo of Matsumae were ordered to survey the distances to the east and west, and in 1648 a Japanese map was produced which showed Ezo, Sakhalin, and the Kurile Islands separately. But the Matsumae fief's contribution to Japanese knowledge of the area was limited. Secrecy, incompetence, and lack of interest were no doubt factors in this failure. However, the fief did establish fishing stations on Sakhalin from 1672, and by 1700 there were reported to be twenty-two Japanese settlements there.

One of the first Japanese works on Ezo was *Ezo Dan Hikki* (Notes on Ezo) by the famous scholar Arai Hakuseki, which was published in the early eighteenth century. This, however, contained little in the way of geographical information. He recorded that the distance from Ezo to the seal rookeries in the Kurile islands was not known, and he did not know of any Japanese having been there. In fact, the area was not entirely unknown to Japanese seamen. Because of Japan's policy of seclusion, they were normally employed only on coastal shipping between Edo and Osaka, but occasionally, because of storms and typhoons, they were driven northwards and wrecked on the coasts of Ezo, the Kuriles, and even Sakhalin. Few ever got back to Japan, and if they did, they were often imprisoned because they had, even if inadvertently, broken the seclusion laws of the shogunate. In any case they were not trained surveyors or cartographers, and they contributed little to Japanese knowledge of the area.

However, even the blinkered government of the Tokugawa shogunate could not totally ignore the increasing Russian interest in the area. As early as 1643 the Cossack Polyarkof is reported to have reached the mouth of the Amur River, from which he could see Sakhalin. In 1706 the Russians took possession of the southern half of Kamchatka, and a Cossack revolt in 1711 led to the discovery of the Kurile Islands. One of the Cossack leaders, Ivan Kosirewskoi, was twice in the Kuriles, in 1712 and 1713, but he got only as far as Paramushir, which is near the top of the chain of Islands. Johann Baptist. Homann (1633–1724) drew a map of Kamchatka and Ezo sometime between 1716 and 1724 which, despite confusion between the two territories, showed progress on earlier maps. A map by Jean Baptiste Bourgignon d'Anville (1697–1782) in

1734, based on reports by J.F. Gerbillons, who had accompanied the commission set up by the Emperor Kangxi to regulate the Chinese border with Siberia, showed the length of Kamchatka and the fact that it was not connected with Ezo. The second expedition of the explorer Bering in 1732 was given the task of exploring Kamchatka from the south. In 1738 a Russian expedition under Captain Spangberg followed the Kurile chain and landed at 38°41′ north and 38° 52′ north on the Japanese coast, while Lieutenant Walton, who had been parted from him in a storm, landed at 38° 17′ north. Some of the results of the expedition were reflected in a map of 1750 by Delisle. Even so, Russian knowledge of the area was far from complete or accurate. A map purporting to summarize European knowledge of Ezo up to that time was produced in 1754 by Philippe Buache, but it did little more than perpetuate earlier errors. Matsumae was, for instance, still shown as a separate island. In fact, the Europeans realized the true shape of Ezo only when the results of the journeys of La Pérouse, Broughton, and Krusenstern were absorbed.

In the meantime the shogun's government finally accepted that it must survey the area if they wished to retain it in the face of Russian expansionism, although the shogunate had resisted for many decades. The map of Ezo published by Hayashi Shihei of Sendai in his *Sankoku Tsuran Zusetsu* in 1758 (An Illustrated Introduction to Three Countries, Pl. 92; the other two countries were Korea and the Ryukyu Islands) was suppressed and the printing blocks destroyed while Hayashi was thrown into prison on the grounds that publication of the book was an offense against the seclusion policies of the government. One factor in this decision may have been that Hayashi referred to a book on geography shown to him by the head of the Dutch factory at Deshima when Hayashi visited Nagasaki in 1777–78. Copies of Hayashi's book nevertheless seem to have reached Europe, as it was translated into French and published by J. Klaproth in 1832. Other Japanese travelers and geographers interested in Ezo and the Kurile Islands included statesman Honda Toshiakira (1744–1821) and Mamiya Rinzō. The latter explored Karafuto and crossed the strait to the mainland in 1808. But the main exploration and survey were carried out by the great Japanese cartographer Inō Tadataka, who was appointed to survey

Ezo in 1800, although his main motive for going to Ezo at this time was to measure accurately a single degree of latitude (see pp. 35–36).

The discovery and exploration of Ezo was thus delayed and haphazard. The Japanese were indeed almost preempted by the Europeans. It is not surprising, therefore, that even in the first half of the Meiji era (1868–1912), Ezo, which was renamed Hokkaido in 1869, was a very backward and underdeveloped area.

Conclusion

The early part of the nineteenth century, following the industrial revolution and the development of world trade, led to increased Western interest in Japan, and attempts to force open the coosed doors of the Tokugawa shogunate gradually intensified. There is no need to repeat here the story of these attempts. One motive was undoubtedly trade, but the growth in shipping in the Pacific also made it essential to find safe havens in Japan for the mariners engaged on the routes which were becoming of increasing importance to the United States in its commerce with China. It was not surprising, therefore, that the door was finally forced open by Commodore Perry and his so-called black ships in 1853. The opening was at first little more than a tiny crack, but the establishment of the United States consulate at Shimoda and the appointment of Townsend Harris as the first United States representative in Japan spelled the end of the seclusion policy. The British, the Dutch, the French, and the Russians quickly followed up, and the so-called Treaty Ports were opened. Shimoda, then a remote spot at the tip of the Izu Peninsula, was abandoned, and Kanagawa was chosen as the port for settlement much nearer to the shogun's capital at Edo. But the shogunate regarded this as indeed too close for its own safety and, it said, that of the foreigners. Instead they developed a settlement at Yokohama which it hoped could be sealed off rather as Deshima in Nagasaki had been for the last two centuries. This hope proved vain. Foreign consulates were established—not only at Yokohama but also at Nagasaki and Hakodate and later at Hyōgo (Kobe) and, for a time, at Niigata—which became the Treaty Ports. The shogun's government was also forced to accept diplomatic missions in the capital of Edo itself. The legations there faced some dangerous and uncomfortable moments in the early 1860s, and most moved temporarily to Yokohama. But by the Meiji Restoration in 1868 Japan was firmly open to the West, although total freedom to travel outside the Treaty Ports had to wait until the revision in the 1890s of the unequal treaties forced by the Western powers on Japan in the mid-nineteenth century.

As we have seen, the cartography of the Japanese islands had been largely established by Inō Tadataka and Western explorers by the early part of the nineteenth century, and this brief account of old maps of Japan, Japanese and Western, should really end there; but history is a gradual development, and there is no absolute dividing line between the old maps and the new scientific cartography. Inō's maps were reissued by the Meiji authorities. Panoramic and old-fashioned route maps were still produced. The new foreign settlements, especially Yokohama, attracted Japanese artists, whose prints depicting the foreigner were in great demand in those days when there were no Japanese newspapers and the Japanese wanted to know what sort of people the foreigners were. Panoramic maps of the Yokohama settlement (Pl. 91) can thus be found among the earlier so-called Yokohama prints.

The Meiji authorities were determined to modernize Japan. Foreigners were employed as experts and teachers, and Japanese went abroad in increasing numbers to study. New, more accurate, and more detailed surveys were undertaken, and maps with contour lines and other Western features were produced. The new Meiji maps are primarily of interest as historical documents, rather than as the works of art so many earlier maps were. They provide, however, fascinating pictures not only of the growth of Japanese towns and cities, but also of communications, in particular the railways. The first railway, between Yokohama and Tokyo, opened in 1872, and in the next three decades railways spread all over Japan.

Even twentieth-century maps are not without interest in this respect. While old railways have fallen into disuse, new lines have sprung up. The railway line to Shimoda in the Izu Peninsula was not, for instance, completed until some years after the Second World War, and the first "bullet-train" (Shinkansen) was not opened until 1964, the year of the Tokyo Olympics. The 1960s, 1970s, and early 1980s also saw the development of the new highway network which, together with reclamation of land and the removal of mountains, has made major changes not only to the landscape but also to the shape of Japan.

The story of old maps of Japan has many facets. Old maps illustrate the history of Japan and its relations with the world outside. They also show the slow growth of geographical knowledge and, in particular, the extraordinary ignorance until early modern times of the area to the north of Honshu. Many old maps are also of artistic merit, and some, such as the gold-leaf folding screens and the woodblock prints, are bona fide works of art. But to me, the most fascinating element has been the interrelationship, or, as the American cartographer Kiss calls it, the crossfertilization, of cultures that has played such a crucial role in the mapping of Japan. It is this feature which has, I think, been sometimes neglected or underplayed in some of the many works in Japanese and foreign languages on old maps of Japan. There is little, for instance, in books in Western languages about the indigenous growth of mapmaking in Japan, and men like Inō Tadataka are much less well known than they should be by Western historians of cartography. But in Japan, too, writers have sometimes seemed to regard Western maps of Japan as simply quaint depictions whose prime interest is that they show how ignorant the foreigners were of Japan. Alternatively, Western maps, including those of Kaempfer and Siebold, are regarded as mere copies of Japanese orginals. Inō Tadataka, it has even been suggested, developed his methods of survey entirely on his own. His devotion to his task and his inventive genius cannot be doubted, but he did not work in a vacuum.

I have not been able in this short work to trace all the crosscurrents of knowledge and influence involved in the development of old maps of Japan, but I hope that I have been able to point out some of the main elements and will have aroused the general interest of others in a subject which has tended in the past to be the preserve of specialists.

64

Plates and Commentaries

1. *Shōen* (estate) map of Minase Manor in Settsu Province. Manuscript, dated 756, 28.5×69 cm, Shōsō-in, Nara. The Minase Manor once belonged to the Tōdai-ji, in Nara. Fields, storehouses, houses, and the village compound are marked on this pictorial map. The manor is ringed by mountains painted in ink. Rice terraces on several levels rise up the slopes on the western perimeter of the manor. The character for east at the top of the map orients the reader.

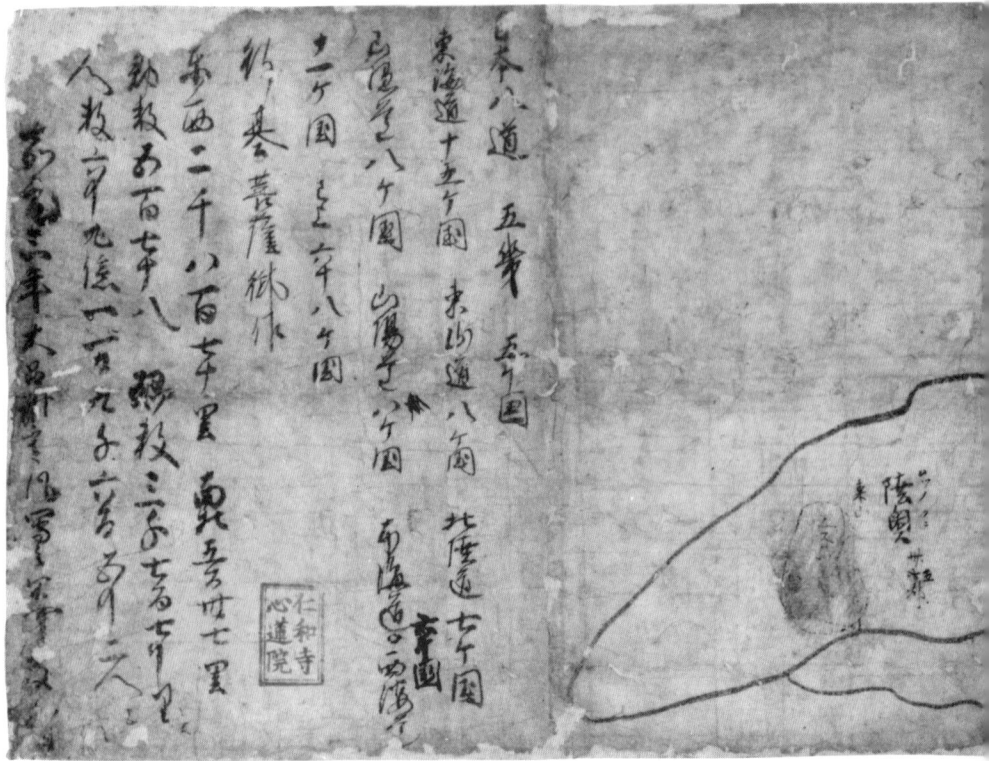

2. Gyōgi-type map. Manuscript, dated 1305, 34.5 × 121.5 cm, Ninna-ji, Kyoto. Much of western Japan is missing, and south is at the top of this early map. The faint lines crossing through the provinces represent early routes, and the text accompanying the map lists the provinces of Japan.

3. Diagram showing the interrelationship of the provinces. Manuscript, early fourteenth century, 22.6 × 30.3 cm, Maeda Ikutokukai, Tokyo. This depiction of the provinces in schematic form appears in the *Nichūreki*, a gazetteer first produced in 1128 and regularly reissued thereafter. North is at the top of the diagram, and the shapes of Honshu, Shikoku, and Kyushu can be roughly made out.

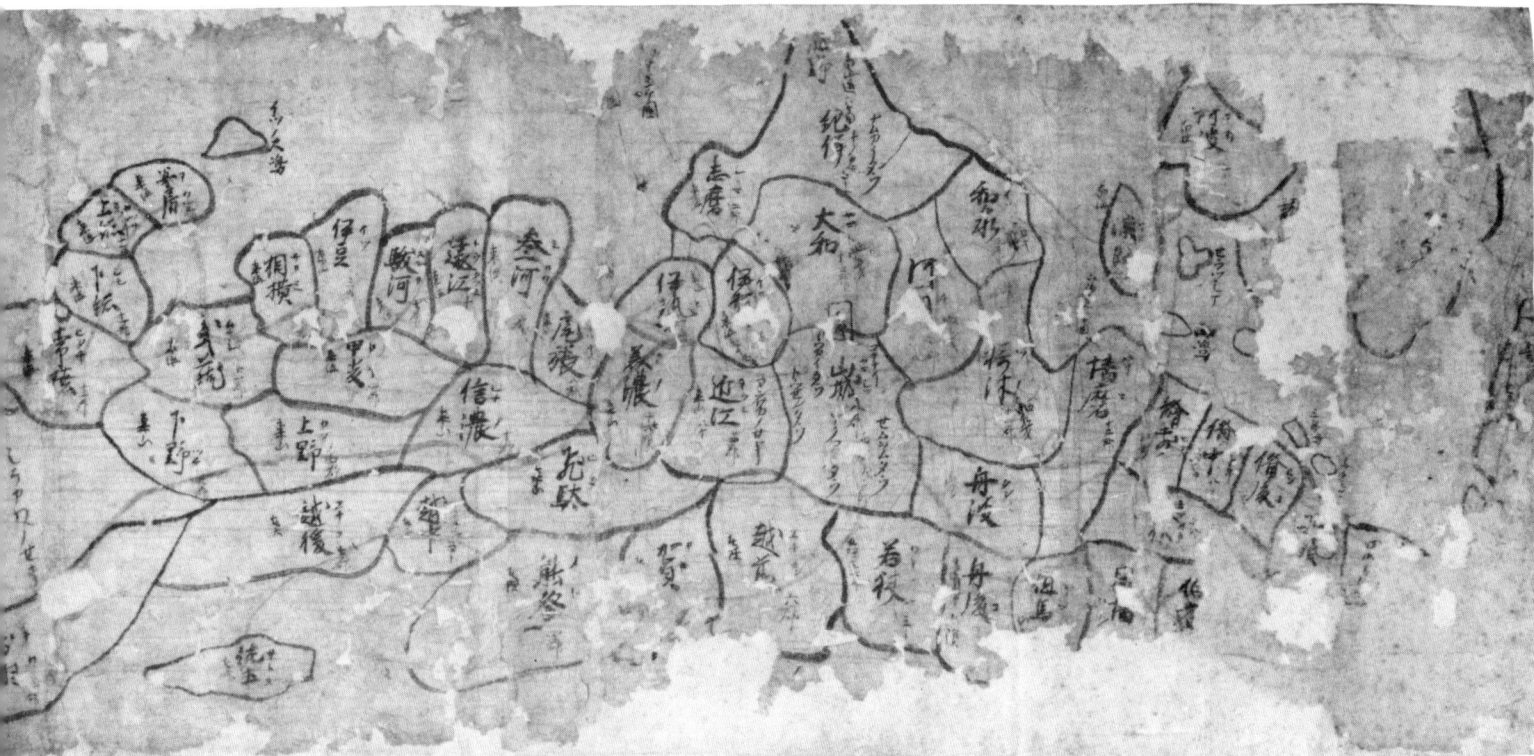

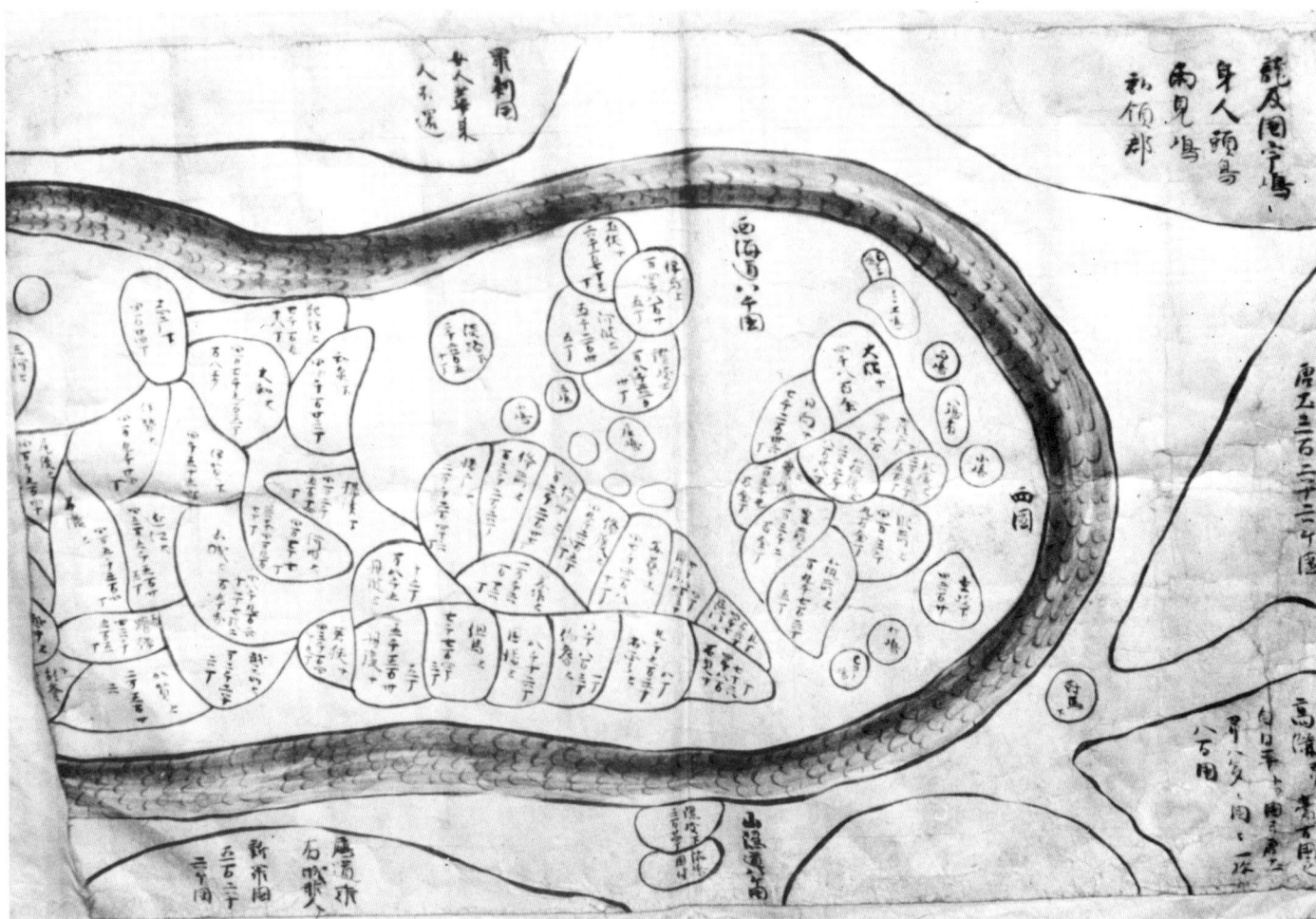

4. Gyōgi-type map. Manuscript, dated 1305, 34×52 cm, Shōmyō-ji possession, Kanazawa Bunko. On this early map, south is again at the top; this time, part of eastern Japan is omitted. Rasetsukoku appears at the upper left, Tang China to the right, and the Korean kingdoms at the bottom border of the map. Japan is wrapped in the coils of a dragon.

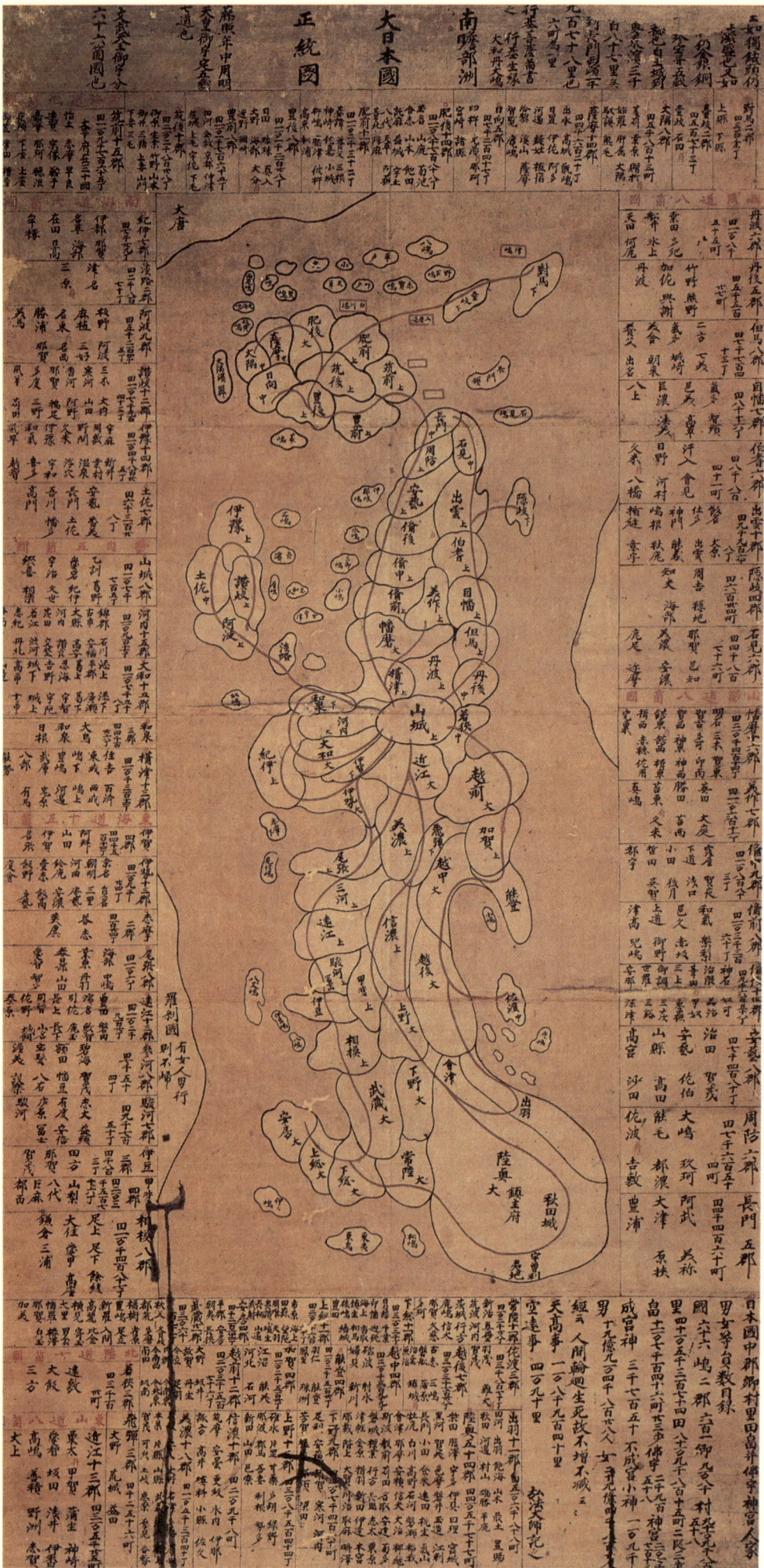

5. *Nansembushū Dainihon Shōtōzu* (Authorized Map of Great Japan and the World). Manuscript, ca. 1557, 168.3 × 85.4 cm, Tōshōdai-ji, Nara. West is more or less at the top of this scroll. The large circle in the midsection, from which red route lines diverge, represents the capital region. Kyushu appears in the upper left section, with a sprinkling of smaller islands separating it from China. The coastline of Rasetsukoku projects from the lower left border of the map. The caption says; "Rasetsukoku, [the land of] women. Men who go there never return." Around the perimeters of the map is a listing of the provinces, districts, and fiefs of Japan. The map is credited to Gyōgi Bosatsu.

6. Gyōgi-type map. Woodblock ▶ print, 27.5 × 17.5 cm, Tenri Central Library, Nara. This map appears in the *Shūgaishō*, a gazetteer first produced in 1291. The date of this early printed copy is uncertain. It is similar in outline and orientation to the map in Plate 5, and also features route lines. Because this map was designed to be read from any direction, the legend is written in one direction and the characters identifying the provinces in another.

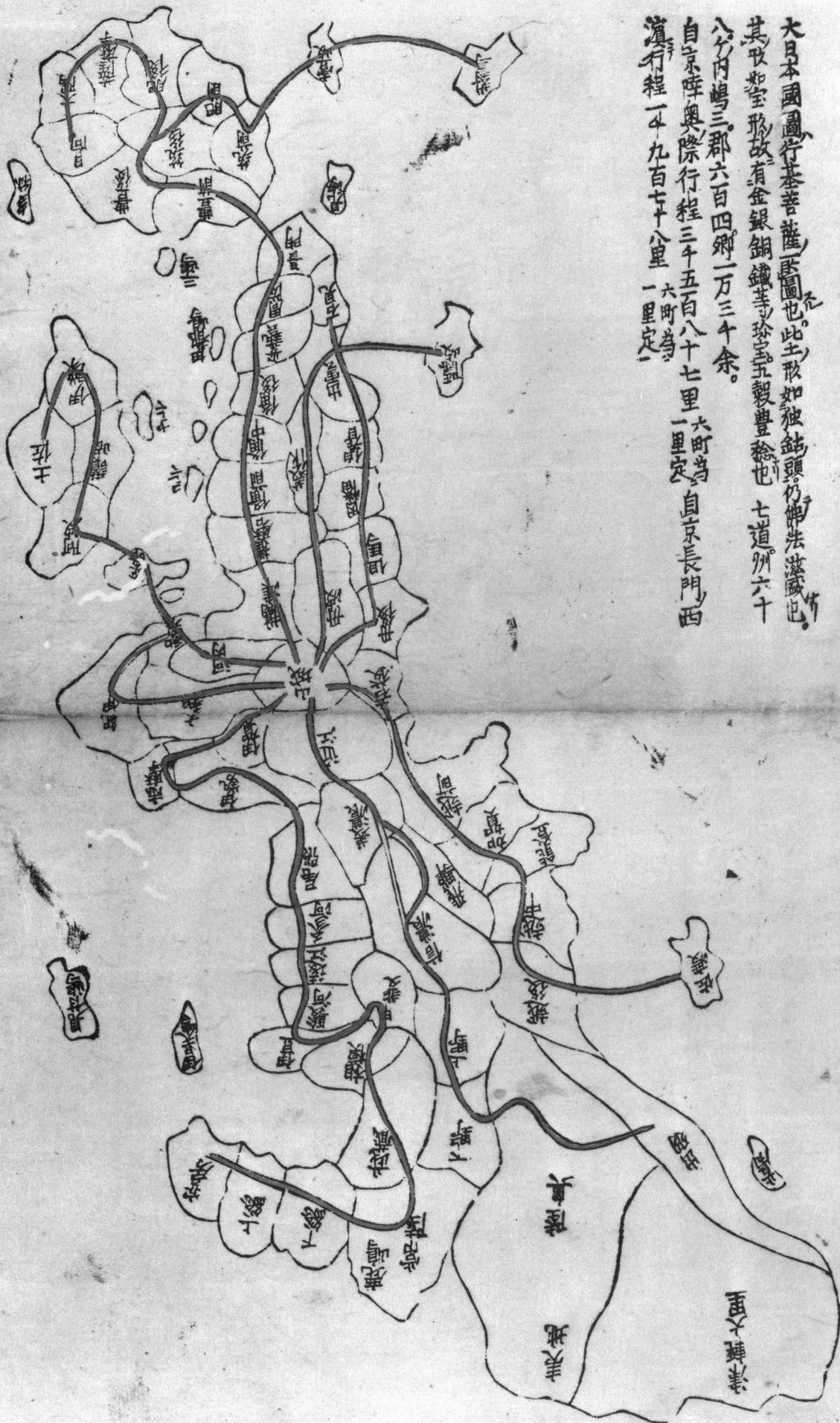

大日本國圖行基菩薩ノ圖也。此ノ土ノ形如獨鈷頭。仍テ佛法滋盛也。

其故ニ寶室形故有金銀銅鐵等ヲ珍寶ヲ五穀豐穣也。七道州六十

八ヶ内嶋三郡六百四郡一万三千余。

自京辛酉奧際行程三千五百八十七里 大町ヲ 六町ヲ 一里定 自京長門西

濱行程一十九百七十八里 一里定一

7. Gyōgi-type map on a *tsuba* (sword guard). Edo period, 8.3×
7.6 cm, Namban Bunkakan, Osaka. Japan is cleverly distorted
to fit on this oval hand guard for a Japanese sword. Stylized
waves separate the islands, which are depicted as Gyōgi-type
"balloons." Tokyo Bay can be seen at right center.

8. Gyōgi-type map on an *inrō* (medicine case), front and reverse. Edo period, 7.1×8.2×2.6 cm, Namban
Bunkakan, Osaka. The front (right) side of the case shows Matsumae and Rasetsukoku in addition to the
northeastern half of Honshu. The reverse (left) side shows southwestern Honshu, Shikoku, and Kyushu.

9. Gyōgi-type map on netsuke. Edo period, 3.5(d)×1.6 cm, Namban Bunkakan, Osaka. All of Japan is crammed in Gyōgi style onto the surface of this ivory netsuke.

10. Gyōgi-type map on Imari-ware plate. Edo period, 28.3×31.8 cm, Namban Bunkakan, Osaka. In addition to Japan, Korea, the Ryukyus, and Rasetsukoku, a "Land of Dwarves" is shown on this plate, at top center.

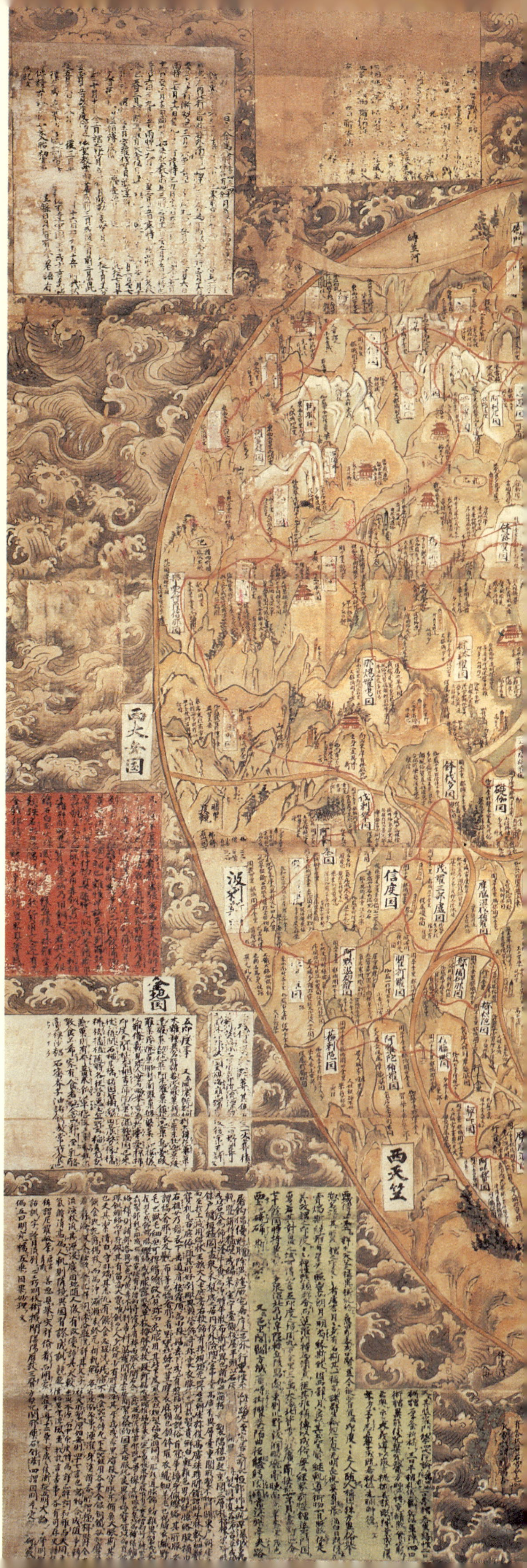

11. *Gotenjikuzu* (Map of the Five Regions of India). Manuscript, dated 1364, mounted as a scroll, 177×166.5 cm, Hōryū-ji, Nara. This traditional Buddhist depiction of the civilized world (mainly India and the Himalayan regions, with a token nod to China) divides India into five regions: north, east, south, west, and central India. Each of these regions is again divided into many kingdoms—those current during the career of the Buddha. The Himalayas are shown as snow-capped peaks in the center of the map, and Mt. Sumeru, the mythical center of the cosmos, is depicted in a whirlpool-like form. A much-reduced China (Chang'an is visible on the plain at the upper right) is labeled "Great Tang." Directly across from China, over the stormy seas, the islands of Kyushu and Shikoku and the form of Honshu can be detected.

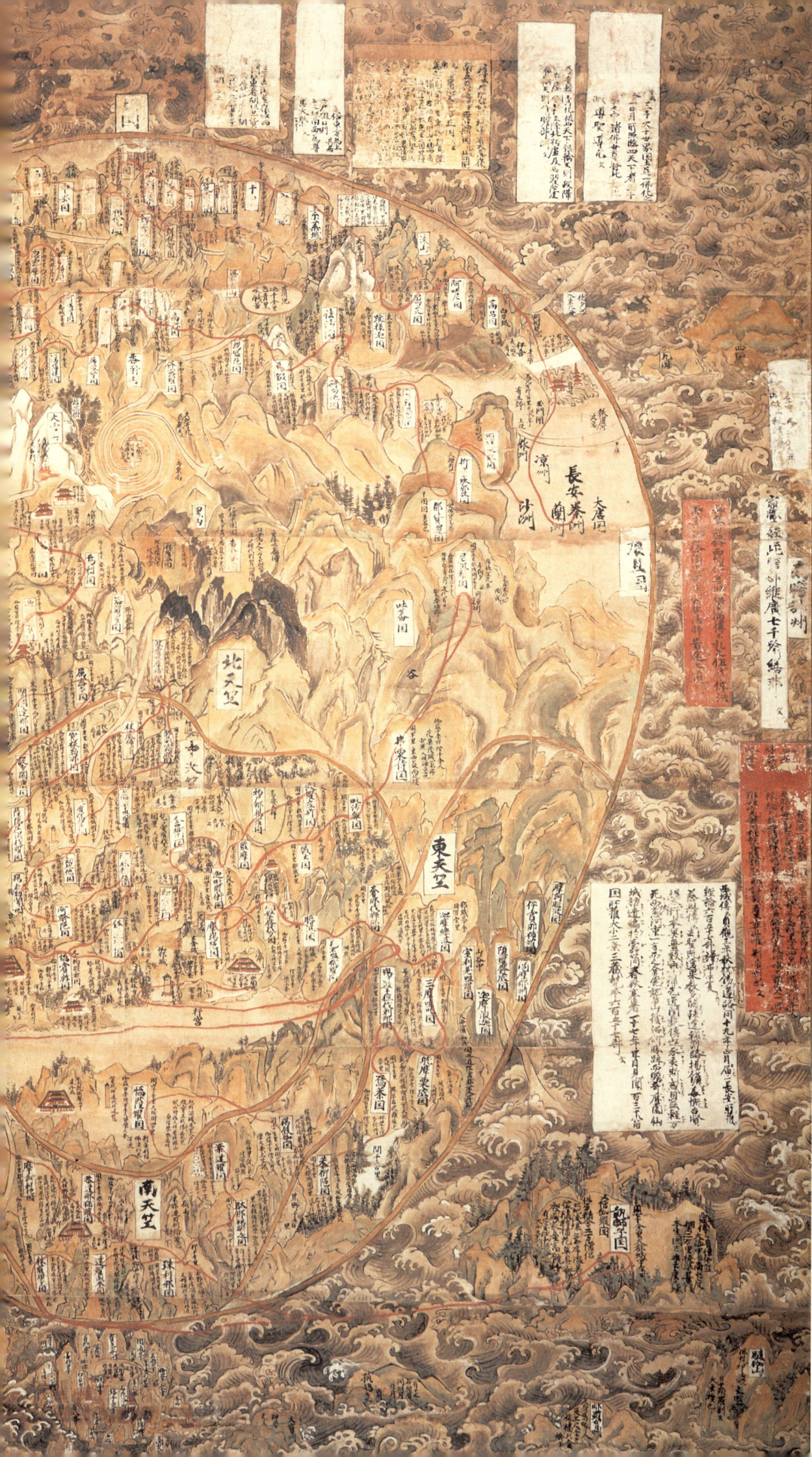

75

La table des Isles neufues, lefquelles on appelle isles d'occident & d'Indie pour diuers regardz.

12. Sebastian Münster: *Die Nüw Welt*. Atlas leaf, 1540, 25.6 × 34.3 cm, Kobe City Museum. Münster's map of the New World was printed in the *Cosmographiae Universalis*, a version of Ptolemy's atlas, published in Basle. Japan appears under the name Zipangri.

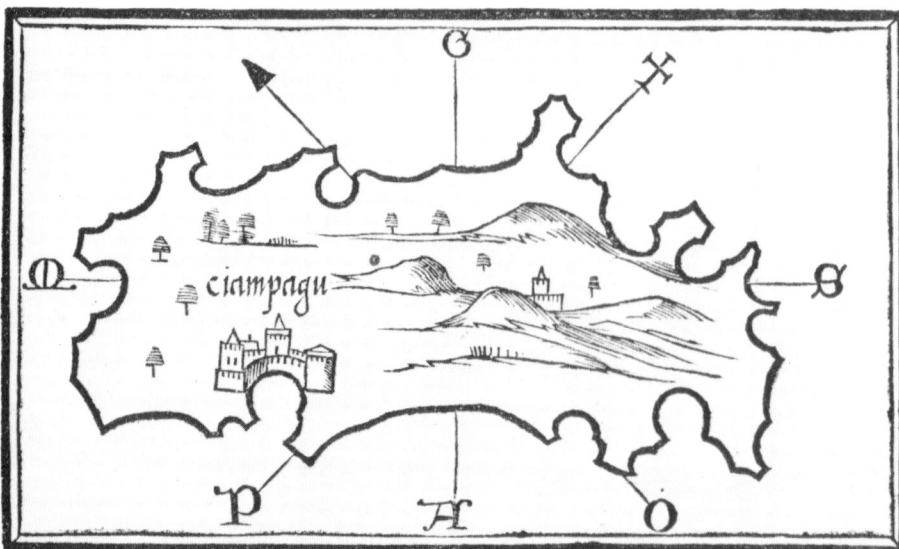

13. Benedetto Bordone: *Ciampagu*. Book leaf, 8 × 14.5 cm, author's collection. Bordone's map first appeared in his *Isolario*, published in 1528.

15. Diogo Homem: part of a map of Asia ▶ showing Japan. Manuscript, 1558, 78.2 × 54.6 cm, British Library, London.

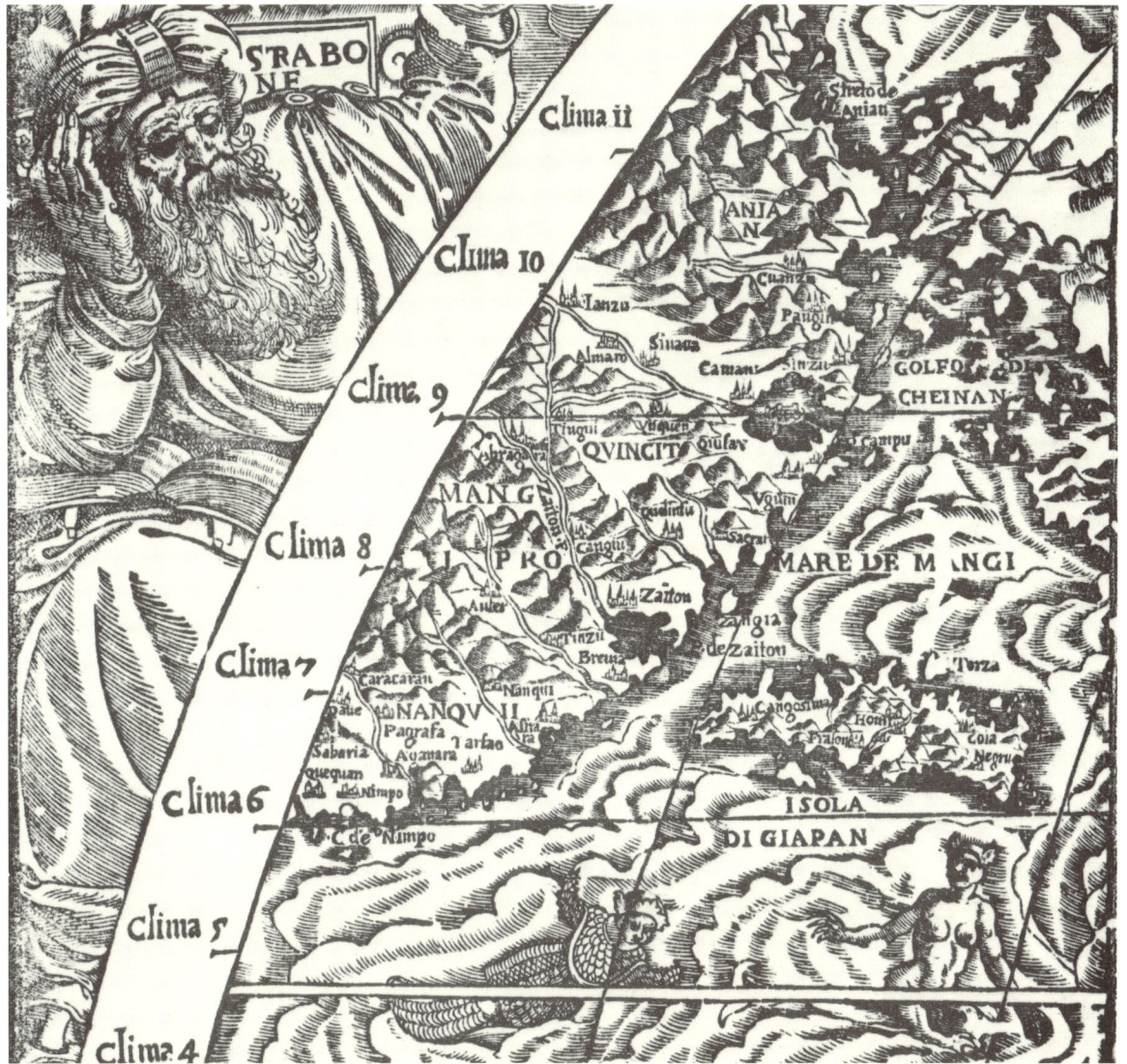

14. Giacomo Gastaldi: *Isola di Giapan*. Atlas leaf, 1562, 25.4×20.3 cm, British Library, London. This is part of Gastaldi's world map, which was first published in Venice in 1546.

16. Abraham Ortelius: *Tartariae Sive Magni Chami Regni Typus*. Atlas leaf, 35 × 47 cm, author's collection. This map of Asia first appeared in the *Theatrum Orbis Terrarum*, published in 1570 in Antwerp. It is particularly interesting for its depiction of the Straits of Anian, first mentioned by Marco Polo.

TAR TARIAE SIVE MAG NI CHAMI REGNI typus

OCEANVS SCYTHICVS
dulcis est Plinio auctore, qui multas in eo
insulas esse dicit, vt etiam M. Paul: Venetus: sed neuter neq, situm neq, numeru tradit.

AMERICAE VEL NOVI OR BIS PARS

ORIENS

Septicum prom.
Danorum
siue Danitarum
hordæ, deiecti siue
asseruso aut depulsi.

Nepthalit arū
horda, Nephthalit.

Tibil locus.

Turbonis horda.

Mecrito
um horda.

BARGV
regio palus
ris

TABOR
REG.

CHIORSA
Caracora
um

DE SERTA
BELGIAN.

ARSARETH
ANIA

ARGON.

Rio Tiguar

Sierra Neuada

Rio de Asa

Chicuich

Tiguas

Coana

Totonteas

Chica na.

P. Primero.

Mar Vermeio

C. Californias

Cazones.

Quinsai id est
ciuitas cæli

QVINCI

MANGI fu.

XAN TON.

NANQVI.

CATAIO.

Cambalu
metropoli

TAIN FV.

Tabin Prom: Plin.

STRETTO DI ANIAN

MARE CIN.

JAPAN.

BVNGO.

Meaco

TONSA.

Japan insula, à M. Paulo
Veneto Zipangri dicta,
olim Chryse, à Magno
Cham olim bello petita
sed frustra.

y. del rio ro.

Ysola di Cedri

y. delle perle

La farfana

Volcani del fuego

Lanieu.

CHEQVAN.

Isola di fogo

7. Islas

Lequino grande

Isola fermosa

Laim

Dos hermanos

MOIN.

CHINA.

Chincheo.

Rocha partida

S. Bartholomeo.

17. Abraham Ortelius: *Indiae Orientalis Insularumque Adiacientium Typus*. Altas leaf, dated 1570, 19.5 × 34.5 cm, author's collection. Japan is shown as an oval main island with chains of smaller islands to the north and south. Mermaids, whales, and sea monsters are sporting in the Pacific between Japan and America.

AMERICAE, Siue Indię Occidentalis pars

Quiuira

Cicuic

Tiguex

Mare Cin

Satyrorum inf.

Inf: de Miaco

Torza

Chela

Saendeber

Bandu

academia

Zangia ins.

Pilbo

Campu

Dinlai

Homi

Amaguco

IAPAN.

Malao

Negru

Hormar

Frason

Canagxina

Menlai

Hanc insulam M.Paul: Venet Zipangri vocat.

OCEANVS

Liampo opr: et proui:

Chequeam

Lequio maior

v.a Fermosa

Reix magos.

Alazacar

Los dos hermanos

Los Bolcanes.

Lequio minor

v.a de benjaga

Tropicus Cancri

Lalabrigo

La farfana

ORIENTALIS

Restinga de ladrones.

Humunu vel y.a di buoni segni.

Zamal

ARCHIPELA: GO DIS.

Inf: de los corales.

Los iardines.

Baia de innocentes.

Hanhan

Panay das

Ceilon

Aguada

Cenalo.

Hibusson

Culuan

Philippina

Pafaie de S.Clara

Abarien.

Huinangan

y.a de mata: lotes

Palohan

Cataram

Ladriot

Cimbubon

Paulogon

Chippit

Mindanao

Buran

y.a de arrecifes

y.a de cocos

LAZA: RO.

Loson

Chippit

Cauit

Candigar

Cabino

Ma-Talao, aliis Tarrao insulę

Doy

Insulę Molucce celebres ob maximā aromatum copiam, quam per totum terrarū orbem transferunt, 5. sunt, iuxta Giloli, nempe Tarenate, Tidore, Motir, Machiā et Bachiā

Taquimar

Sanguin

Morotay

Tarenate

Gilolo

Borneo INS.

Bilalon

Babarao

Tamiampura

Calamba

Supa

Celebes

Mamon

Manada

Guehe

Circulus æquinoctialis.

v.a de crespos.

y.a de los martires

Cainam

Macace

Pulola: or.

Bandan

Caylan

Am:

Arui

NOVA GVINEA quam Andreas Corsalus Ter: ram Piccinaculi appellare vi: detur. An insula sit, an pars continentis Australis incer: tum est.

Galiam

Timor, Tidore inf:

Alifao

Cimpegua

Sumbdit

Jauegna

BEACH, pars inentis Australis.

Jap

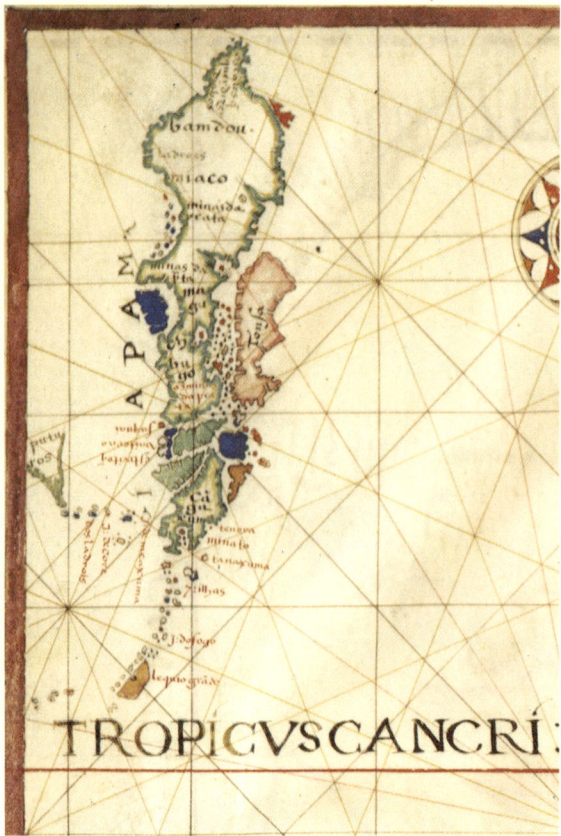

18. Bartolomeu Velho: *Iapam*. Manuscript, 1560, 41.5×30.2 cm, Henry E. Huntington Library, San Marino, California.

19. Abraham Ortelius: *Asiae Nova Descriptio*. Atlas leaf, ca. 1567, 37×48.6 cm, Tenri Central Library, Nara. Japan is shown in the shape of a large tadpole in this map, which is quite distinct from the Ortelius map in Plate 17.

Prom: Scythicum
Ciremisso: rum horda
Turbarum horda
Turb lac
Yezucanorud horda
Vaigatz
Chiesanoru horda
Mecritorum horda
BARGV regio palustris
Taigin

Parall 80 Borealis
Parallel 70 Borealis
Parallele 60 Borealis
Parall 50 Borealis
Parall 40 Borealis
Parall 30 Borealis
Parall 20 Borealis
Parall 10 Borealis

MARE SCYTHICVM
TABIN Plinius et M. P. Venetus multas in eo insulas esse dicunt, sed numerum & situm tradunt.
Insula sabulosa

Tabin Pro:
SARSARETH
Gonzu
Pangin
ANIA
Hic vasa porcellana dicta singuntur
Zizim
Quansii
Vquen
Sinava
Cauzu
Cangu
Quin
ARGON
BELGIAN
Aanzu
Tingu
Curasi
Fungui
Zaiton
Chian
Zardandā

Vrbs Quinsai habet vt M. P. Venetus refert 100 mill: pass: in circuitu, habetque 12.000 pontes.

QVINCI
XANTON
Abragana
Tinzu
Quiensa
Lauton
Sauzu
Laion ft:
Brema
PANDVMIA
IAPAN Insula
Osaqui
Mensa da prata
Oxor
Afeog
COO MAGVCHE
Ea farsana
Volcan del fuego
Laniem
BVNGO
Bungo
TONSA:
Tomas
Ofochima
Cangaxuma
Dos ermanos

TARTARIA
Desertum Apas. tachit
Desertum Caracoram
HIC MAGNOS CHAM TARTARORVM ET CHATHAM IMPERATOR LONGE LATE QVE DOMINATVR
TABOR
CHIORZA
Mons Althay
MA NGI
Guenginsi
Autet
Asinodech Nanqui
Spilo
S. Maria
P. de fogo
Islas
Lain
Taxima
Le------

ENAHER
Desertum Caracoram
Socharifi:
TVRCH
CIARCIAN
Lop
TANGVT
Suceuir
Caracora
Cambalu Cataie metropolis
Cambalu habet 28 mill: pass: in circuitu
Pons marmoreus 300 passus
TAINFV
Tesfur
Singui
Tainfu
Cinda
YANQVI
P. de Fermosa Reis magos

Hic habaharū tanta copia prouenit vt hinc ad omnes orbis partes vehatur

OCEANVS EOVS. siue orientalis

DVCH
CATA IO
Pilico
CHEQVAN
Cū de Lampo
Lequibo pequinho
Lequibo grande

TEN
Sachion
CAMVL
Cumul
CAINDV
Thebet
SINDINFV
Cianba
THEET
Cipribi
Mozu
Pazanfu
Gingui
MOIN
CHINA
Maisan
Bengatera
Abroio

ERGIMVL
Erginul
Lac Salsus
CARDANDAN
CARAIAN
Cachobaih
Guanzu
Matan
Auada
Bemaga

INDOS
India intra Gangem
TANGVT
Imaus mons
Iuontio
MACIN
Torsals
Singoua
Tipura
Ciou
Chenchi
Igao

MENDAO
Coloma
Mem
TIPVRA
Cintingui
Tholoman
GAVCINCHI NA
Cachiu
Pontoa
Los Iardinos
Los Corales
La Barbuda
Elhas dos Reis
Carime na
Ilhas de hombres blancos

ORISSA
PIDIR
BENGAIA Bengala
VERMA
Bacalla A VIA
Langoma
CAMPAA
Canpha
Pulorstan
Daria
Maracaon
Dr Cabos
Matelotes
Arizifes
I. de Abrigo
Darimo
Doarti
Maoo
R. de S. Lorenzo
R. de S. Augustino

GOLFO II
Basse
PEGV
Baato
Donga
Yara
CAMBOIA
Cambria Brardm
Taubona tella
Porcmeli
C. Losa
Mindano
Porto Cataia
Palme
Alhas de S. Iohan
L. dos crespos
L. dos Martilez

BENGA LA
Andemahon
Odia
Pisan
MA: Pusilola
LA: CA:
Lungura
Andamon
Palo han
Gaida
Mompialst
Ma nilha
L. de S. Ioan
Nalabo
Stevenata
Panca ian
L. Dider
Cai stan
C. Hermoso
NOVA GVINEA
Cum Privilegio

ZEILAN
Beligan
Nicobar
Gosmin
Pedir
Achis
Data
Birar
SAMO:
Ciagua
Pietra bianca
Narleua
Tamiandaron
Borneo
Taiapura
Supa
Bura
Cara
Ceia
Cum Privilegio

frole dor
Irolas de Nanacar
TRA olim Taprobana Zonda
Ticos
Bacomana
Linga
Chinabalo
Panagam
Calamba
Damadura
Nusasha
Lucato
Teralta
Altnica bon Sin
Banca
Quirima
IAVA MINOR

JAVA MAIOR
Palimbam

TERRAE INCOGNITAE AVSTRALIS PARS
Parall 10 Australis
Parall 20 Australis

ORIENS

20. Fernão Vaz Dourado: map of Asia showing Japan. Manuscript, 1568, 33 × 45 cm, Henry E. Huntington Library, San Marino, California. "Iapam" spills over the border at the upper right of this beautifully colored manuscript.

FIRME D TARTARIA

IAPAM

LIAMPO

REINOS DA
CHINA

TROPICVS

CANCER

RACŌ

PEGV

SIAM

Map text (on the map):

ASIAE PARS ORIENT.

Tartariæ li= mites.

In China regione, Iapania aliisque insulis vicinis, messis multa Christianorum: quorum indies novæ coloniæ ducuntur, patribus societatis Iesu fidis operarijs.

AMERICAE

Quivira

TRIONALI

Murus quingentorum leucar

Xanton

Paquin

CHINAE REGNI PARS

C. Liamton

Isla de Plata.

Argyra hęc forte antiquorum.

Grandes corrientes

R. de los estrecho

C. de Trabaios

C. Mendocino

Costa brava

Cequi.

Molinu

Iapan ins. nuper ad Fidem Christianam conversa.

Hucheo

Foquiem

Y. de Ladrones

Las dos Hermanos

Los Bolcanes

Suadecheo

Cincheo

Malabrigo

La Farfana

Lequeo grande

Circulus Cancri.

MARE

Lequeio pequenno

Islas de Lucois.

Res tiga de ladrones

Cubo

Baxos de S. Bartholemeo

Philippinas.

Y. de Sto

CUM,

Dos Arcifes

Los Iardines

Nimoro

Cubo

Dos Matalotes

Y dos Corales

Mindanao

B. de Malage

Y. de los ras

Pracel

Galeo

Terrena

Carangao

Costa de moro

Mal luc ques.

Nova Guinea, quibusdam Terra de Piccinacoli.

Celebes

Caima

La casimana

Isabella

Insulæ Salomonis

Banda

Timor

Iava Mior

Baxos

Tierra baxxa

S. Marcos

Circulus Capr

SPE ET METV.

GENIO ET INGENIO NOBILI DN. NICOLAO ROCCOXIO, PATRICIO ANTVERPIENSI, EIVSDEMQVE VRBIS SENATORI, Abrahamus Ortelius Regiæ Mts geographus lub. merito dedicabat.

15 89

TERRA SIVE MAG DVM D

21. Abraham Ortelius: *Maris Pacifici Novissima Descriptio*. Atlas leaf, 1589, 34×49 cm, Matsutarō Namba Collection, Kobe City Museum. North of a roundish Honshu is depicted an "Isla de Plata," and silver mines are identified in southwest Honshu. Adjacent to the archipelago is the comment: "The Japanese islands are not yet converted to Christianity." Thus, the major European interests in Japan at this time are revealed by this map.

86

MARIS PACIFICI,

(quod vulgò Mar del Zur)
cum regionibus circumiacentibus, insulisque in eodem
passim sparsis, novissima descriptio.

PTEM=

PARS.

50

40

MARIS ATLANTICI,

SIVE MAR DEL NORT

30

PARS.

Bermuda

Florida

Noua Hispania.

Messico

Cuba

Spagnola

Iamaica

S. Ioan

La Trinidad

Cartagena

Caribana.

Quito.

Mar Ver=
mejo

Calit=
Formia

Iss. hermosas
Islas de los Cedros
Islas. de
los diamantes
Y de S.
Thomas
La anublada

Rocca partida.

Y de Cocos

Y. de Galopagos.

Circulus Aequinoctialis.

AMERICAE

MERIDIONA=

LIOR PARS.

Peru.

Charcas.

Chili.

Patagones.

S. Petri.

Prima ego velivolis ambivi cursibus Orbem,
Magellane novo te duce ducta freto.
Ambivi, meritoq; vocor VICTORIA: sunt mi
Vela, alæ; precium, gloria; pugna, mare.

Archipe=
lagus in=
sularum.

Fretum Magella=
nicum.

Mar.
del Nort.

STRALIS,

ANICA, NON=

ECTA.

Cum privilegijs Imp. & Reg. Maiestatum,
nec non Cancellariæ Brabantiæ, ad decennium.

MERIDIES.

Tierra del Fuego.

I F I

O D V V L G O

N O M I = N A N T,

M A R

D E L

Z V R.

22. Arnoldus à Langren (Arnold van Langren):
map of Asia. Book leaf, 1596, 38.4×51.7 cm,
Tenri Central Library, Nara. The map appears
in the account of Linschòten's travels, *Schipvaert
van Ian Huygen Van Linschòten Naer Oost Ofte Por-
tugaels Indien*, published in Amsterdam in 1596.
The depiction of "Iapones" is very similar to
that in Plate 20. East is at the top in this map,
which is notable for its Chinese bestiary and
depiction of Korea as an island.

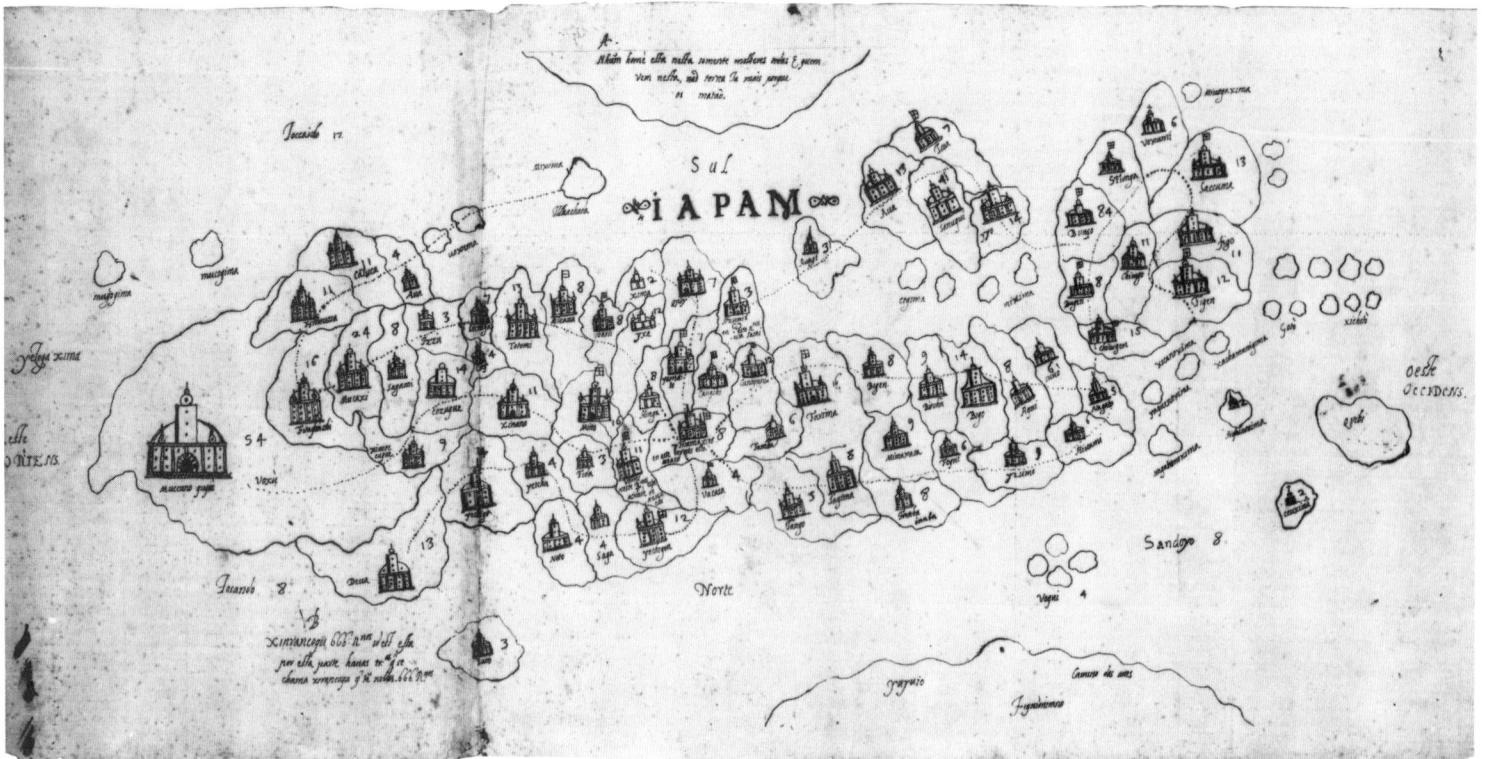

23. Gyōgi-type map of "Iapam." Manuscript, 28×60 cm, Archivio di Stato, Florence. Professor G. Crino of the University of Florence discovered this map among the Medici papers dealing with the East India trade. South (Sul) is at the top in this map. "Yezogaxima" [Ezo] is labeled at the far left.

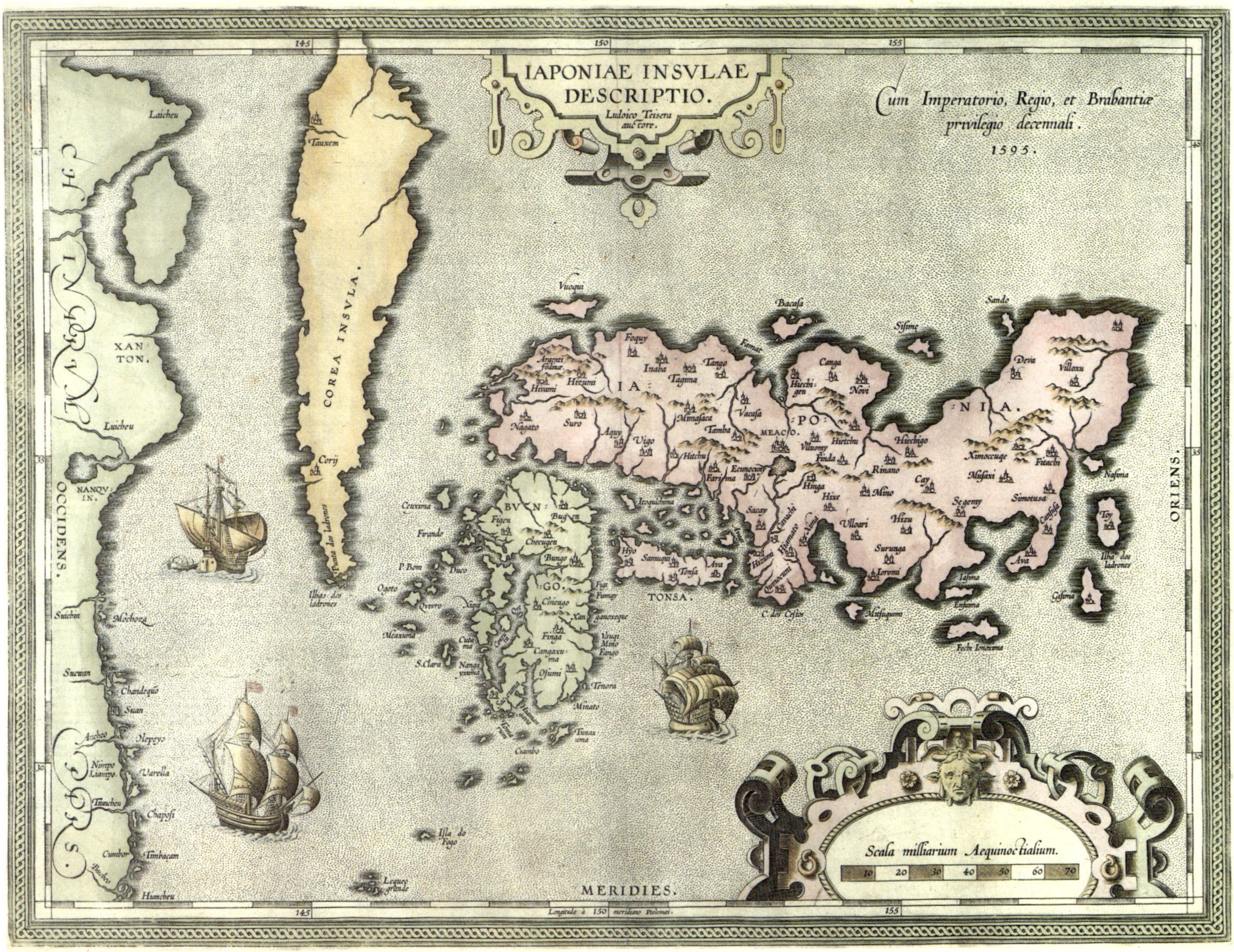
IAPONIAE INSVLAE DESCRIPTIO.
Cum Imperatorio, Regio, et Brabantiae privilegio decennali.
1595.
COREA INSVLA.
XAN TON.
OCCIDENS.
ORIENS.
MERIDIES.
TONSA.
Scala milliarium Aequinoctialium.
10 20 30 40 50 60 70

25. Luis Teixeira: *Iaponiae Insulae Descriptio.* Atlas leaf, 35.5×48.5 cm, author's collection. This map appears in *Additamentium V* (1595) to Abraham Ortelius's *Theatrum Orbis Terrarum*, published in Antwerp, and was to serve as a model for many cartographers. The maps in Plates 26–29 all owe much to Teixeira's depiction of Japan. Of particular interest is the depiction of Korea as an island, and the ''Ilhas dos Ladrones'' off the Korean and Japanese coasts.

◀ 24. Renwart Cysat: *Der grossen namhafften neuwlicherfunden Japponischen Insel.* Book leaf, 26.5×40.6 cm, Tenri Central Library, Nara. Cysat's map was first published in the *Wahrhafftiger Bericht* in Freyburg in 1586. ''Minas de plata'' and other ''minas'' are visible in the north. Place names are hard to identify, but Nagasache [Nagasaki] can be detected at the upper left, and Azuchi, the site of the famous castle, in the lower right section.

28. Abraham Ortelius: *Iaponia Insula*. Atlas leaf, 8 × 10 cm, author's collection. This somewhat simplified version of Teixeira's map was first published in Ortelius's miniature atlas of 1598, in Antwerp.

◄ 26. Mercator-Hondius: *Iaponia*. Atlas leaf, 34×44.5 cm, author's collection. A close copy of Teixeira's map with decorative changes, this map appears in Hondius's reissue of Mercator's atlas, published in Amsterdam in 1606.

◄ 27. Jan Jansson: *Iaponiae Nova Descriptio*. Altas leaf, 33.5×44 cm, author's collection. Jansson reissued Teixeira's map with decorative additions and changes in his *Novus Atlas*, published in Amsterdam in 1646–47.

29. John Speed: *The Kingdome of China*. Atlas leaf, 1626, 39 × 50 cm, author's collection. Even the famous cartographer Speed relied on Teixeira's map, as can be clearly seen in his depictions of Korea and Japan here: Korea remains an island, and the Ilhas dos Ladrones appear off the southern tip of Korea and the eastern coast of Japan. Another interesting feature of this map is the Straits of Anian, separating "Cathaya" and "Parte of America."

A CHINIAN WOMEN

A SOVLDIER OF IAPAN

A CHINIAN

A MEN OF PEGV

the KINGDOME OF CHINA *newly augmented by I.S.* 1626

KINGDOME OF CHINA

PARTE OF INDIA WITHIN GANGES

THE KINGDOME OF BRAMAS.

INDIA WITHOVT GANGES.

BENGALA

THE GVLFE OF BENGALA, Sometymes called THE GVLFE OF GANGES.

SVINAM

CAVCHIN CHINA

Qui - nzay

the Manner of   their Execution

TANGVTH
Out of this Kingdome, men will
haue all Rubarb to be brought
vnto them of Europe.

Camul
Sachion Succuir
This Countrey is a li about
the w.ch Earth is disgest w.th small haires like
grasse, w.ch being spun in or wouen
a clothe therof being cast in
fire is not burst.

Campion y.e chief City of
Tanguth, whose inhabitans
are partly Christians, and
partly Mahumetists.

Cerguth

Gauta
Quiqui
Hoyam Mulon
Suidio

CATHAYA, the
Chief
Kingdome
of Great Cam.

Sandri
R. Pulisanga
Achbaluch
Serra
Gouza
Cambalu
circui
Catlaye
Metropo
Iangio

Ciangli

Cianganor id
est lakus
Albus
Chianca
Xandu
Brema
Xandu

Cambalu Cathaye is in
latitan, is in
łt 28. miles.

A wall of 400 leages, betwixt
the bankes of y.e hilles, built of y.e King of
China against y.e breaking in of y.e Tartars on this side.

THE STRAITE OF ANIAN.

PARTE
OF
AME-
RICA.

C. de Fortuna.

C. Quinchio
C. Tonches
C. Ssoquari
QUIN-
CII
C. Paquin
C. Pautim
Chulisu
Pimpim
Tianchieu
C. Sanci
XIAMA
Tiachio
XII.
Huchio
Cenchio
Pemamhu
Tiancheu
Cienfu
Tiancheuoy
Suntchu
C.Pa.ssmnhu

C. Liamton
Taemchu
Cichio
Tenches
Cinchco
C. de Richeo

A CHINIAN MEN

XAN-
Xuntien
al.
Quinzay
TON.
Temechio
Cheathenu
Lu lun
Sachiuu
Lauchcu
C. Ssichiu

A CHINIAN MEN

Ho.
NAO.
R. Chiam
Pilingu
Saiasfu
C.Na niquin
Nodachiu
NAN
QUII.
CHE-
QVIA.M.
Huneon
Sichio
Tingingiu
Luchiu
Teachio
Molun
Suichin

Pochio
Luichen
oran.
orun

Vuequi
Bacas Ilands
Sisime
Sauls

Lauichu

THE ILE COREA

Cascand de Nanquin.

Taucem

Cory

I. A P A N

A SOVLDIER OF IAPAN

THE   CHINI

AN

Quinihahu
Ouilan
Hujuchiu
Linguou
Chiambuchiii
Quiamhu
Anchee
Huchoun
Buchea

Scautanu
c. Chiquano
Liampu
Chi.anchu

Mochona
Ilhas des
ladrones
Suan
Olepeyo
Varella
chagsi
C. de Liampo
Cimbacam
Limhat

BVN
GO
Finlan
Tonara
Amaxi
Tomeonguai
Tlaxuma
I. Ilands
Tonsa
Las dos Hermosas
Mallabro

Ly
Ilhas dos
Ladrone
Vichi Lenoxima

CII.
Sochio
Lamhic puh
Guiachiu

UCANTAM

Cabaxoia
R. del Sol
Lampeda

Chamhic
Bue.hio
I. Napacu

Ciamho
Nagu rimin

NCII

Ouanlari
Taichin
Tio
Vanchia
I. Inhosa
Ponte d'Aynan
El Pracel
lo S.Polo

Watebi
C. Batacali

Licheni
Chaguas

Lu
Linaon
Aquarius
CO
NIA

Dos Reys Magos
Fermosa
lesser Lequeo
Lequeo grande
I. di Fogo

I. de Siera

Duas Cohmas
Vno Coluna

De Sierta

Baleabriga

OCEAN.

C. del Engano
Corio hermoso
C. Batachi
P. Escondido
P. da Paiores
de Matalonhombre
Hainchii

The Germanian
miles.
The English
miles.

15   30   45   60   75   90
60 120 180 240 300

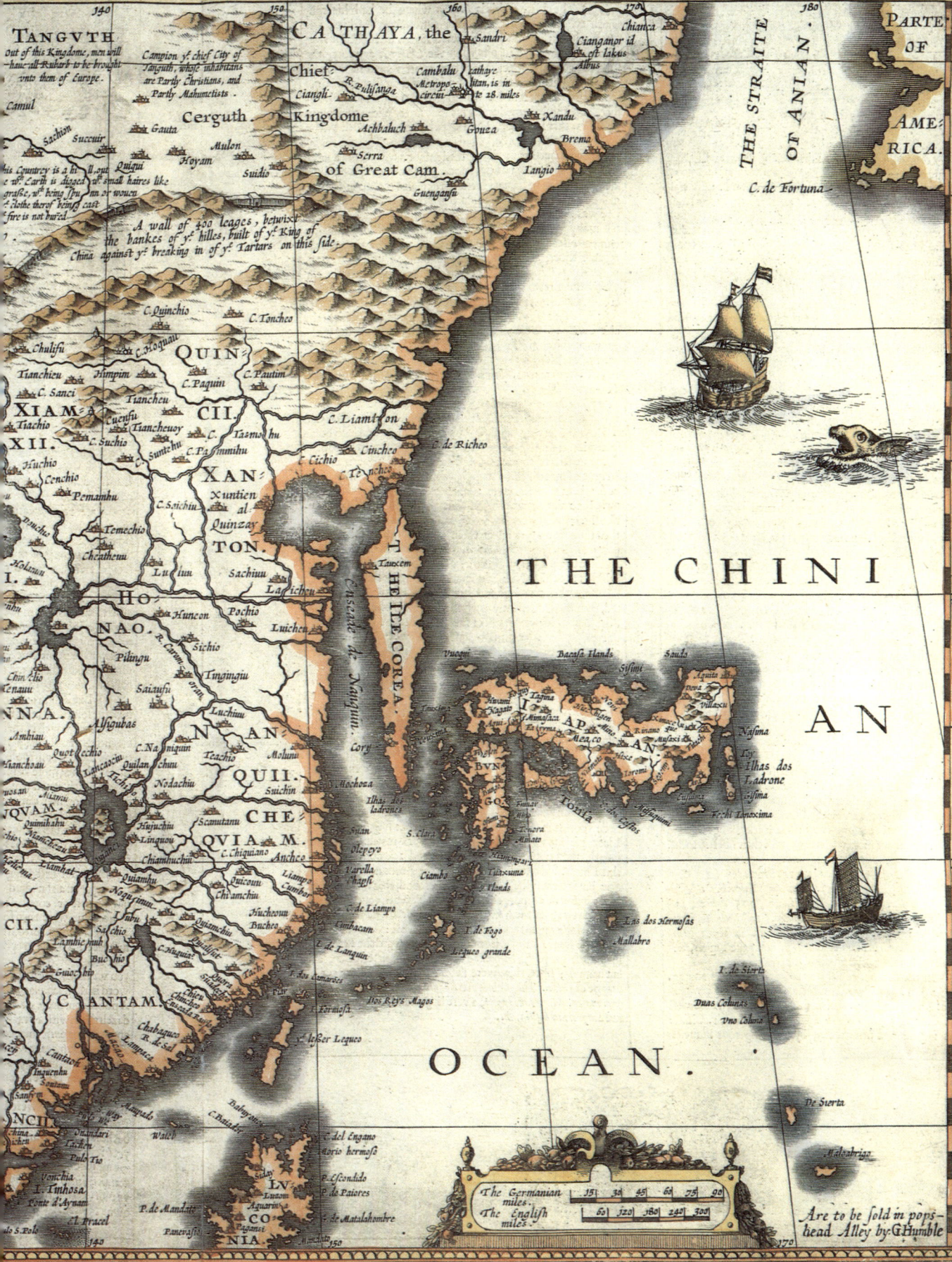

Are to be sold in pops-
head Alley by G. Humble

A WOMEN OF PEGV

95

30. Map of Japan. Manuscript, early seventeenth century, 370 × 433.7 cm, National Diet Library, Tokyo. This map was compiled on the orders of the Tokugawa shogunate in the Keichō era (1596–1614) and was completed towards of the end of the Kanei era (1624–43). Provinces and main cities are marked, along with major routes.

31. Map of the province of Bizen and its nine subdivisions. Manuscript, early seventeenth century, 191 × 186 cm, Okayama University, photograph courtesy of Kodansha, Ltd. The lozenge shapes identify villages and towns.

32. See following foldout ▶

34. *Shinsen Dainihon Zukan* (Revised Map of Japan). Woodblock print, dated 1687, 69.1×92.5 cm, Kobe City Museum. The seal-like impressions, black with white lettering, identify each province by name. The names of the daimyo as well as their stipends in *koku* appear within the boundaries of their respective domains. A list of provinces, districts, villages, temples, shrines, and other administrative units appears at the top, which is north in this map. Korea—Chōsenkoku—protrudes from the upper left border. Ezo, with its fief of Matsumae, is clearly labeled in the extreme upper right, running off the map (conveniently obscuring the relationship of Ezo to the mainland, a matter of some doubt at the time).

35. Map of Japan. Painting, section of a sixfold screen, late sixteenth century, 163.8 × 251.2 cm, Jōtoku-ji, Fukui. This screen and the matching screen in Plate 36 are attributed (questionably) to Kanō Eitoku.

36. Map of the world. Painting, section of a sixfold screen, late sixteenth century, 163.8 × 314 cm. Jōtoku-ji, Fukui. This and the previous screen are in the *kimpeki* style (brilliant colors set against a gold background), and are excellent examples of the gorgeous Momoyama-period (1568–1615) screens.

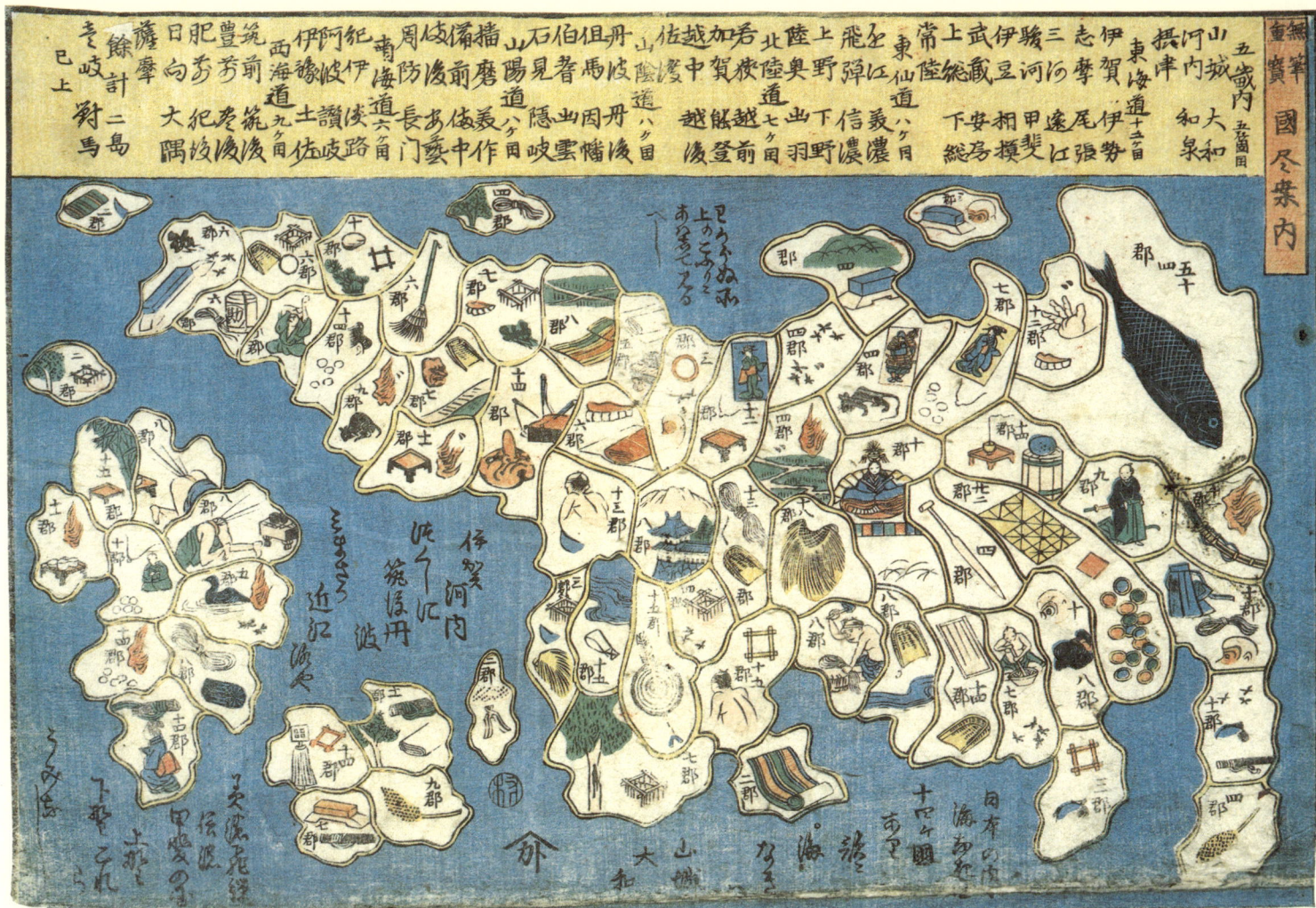

37. *Muhitsu Chōhō Kuni-zukushi Annai* (Convenient Pictorial Guide to the Provinces). Woodblock print, mid-nineteenth century, 26 × 36.4 cm, Kobe City Museum. A sense of fun is evident in this illustrated map, with the names of the provinces in rebus form. The island of Awaji in the Inland Sea is pictured with a spray of millet (*awa*) and a koto bridge (*ji*). The northern province of Echigo is illustrated with a picture (*e*), a woman's breast (*chi*), and a handful of *go* stones. Hyūga in Kyushu is depicted by a fire (*hi*), a cormorant (*u*), and moths (*ga*). Though the map is intended for the illiterate, a good deal of ingenuity is required to decipher the names.

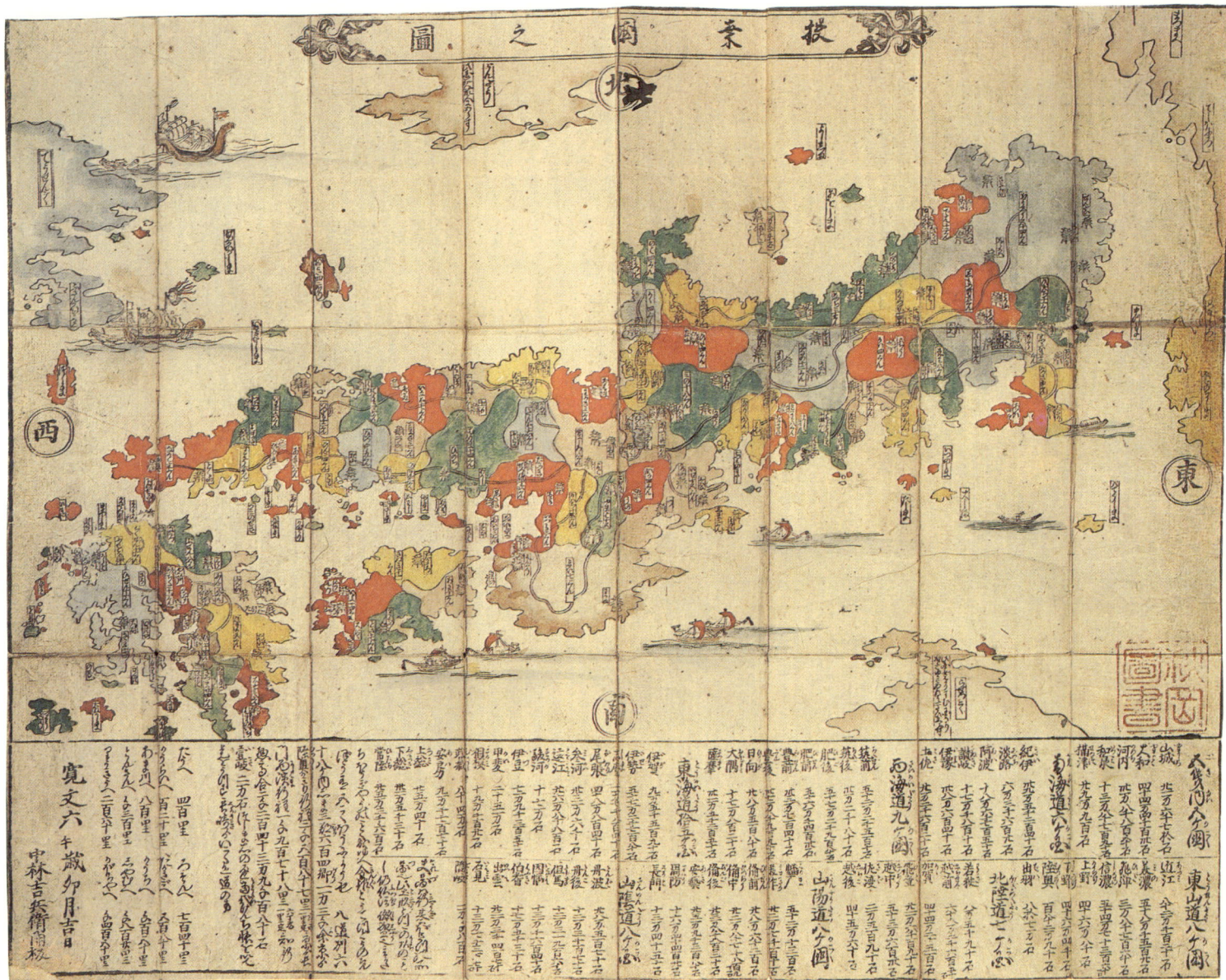

38. Nakabayashi Kichibei: *Fusōkoku no Zu* (Map of the Land of the Rising Sun). Woodblock print, dated 1666, 38.5×49.5 cm, Akioka Collection, National Museum of Japanese History, Sakura-shi, Chiba.

39. Map of Japan with fiefs and *koku* of rice. Woodblock print, late seventeenth century, 69.5×163 cm, author's collection. George Beans (*see* Bibliography) comments on this map: "The Daimyo Ogasawara Daisuke is named on the map, in Buzen. He changed his name to Ogasawara Shūri in December 1683, hence our conjectural date [of 1683]."

40. Mabuchi Jikōan (with Okada Jiseikan): *Kaisei Dainihon Zenzu* (Revised Map of Great Japan). Woodblock ▶ print, ca. 1700, hand-colored, 78.8 × 126.5 cm, Kobe City Museum. The legends on the upper and lower borders of the map contain lists of provinces. Major routes and major and minor post-stations and inns are marked, as well as sea routes and distances in leagues (*ri*).

以上六十八州六百二十八郡

難波陳人
馬關氏自某菴圖
岡田氏貝自有刻書

南海道六箇國

國	管郡	高
紀伊	上管七郡	高四十二万千八百石餘
淡路	上管二郡	高六万四千二百石餘
阿波	上管九郡	高十九万二千九百石餘
讃岐	上管旦郡	高十七万五千百石餘
伊豫	上管四郡	高三十六万七千五百石餘
土佐	中管七郡	高二十六万七千五百石餘

西海道九箇國

國	管郡	高
筑前	上管十五郡	高三十二万千百石餘
筑後	上管十郡	高三十万千餘石
豊前	上管八郡	高三十万六千三百石餘
豊後	上管八郡	高五十六万九千二百石餘
肥前	大管四郡	高五十七万五千七百石餘
肥後	中管四郡	高二十九万三千餘石
日向	中管五郡	高十七万八千二百石餘
大隅	中管八郡	高三十二万五千三百石餘
薩摩	中管四郡	高二十三万五千三百石餘
壹岐	下管二郡	高二万六千九百石餘
對馬	鳴二箇國	高上一萬六千九百石餘

（地図上の國名）
陸奥　出羽　越後　佐渡　上野　下野　信濃　甲斐　駿河　尾張　三河　遠江　近江　山城　伊賀　伊勢　大和　紀伊　河内　摂津　播磨　若狭　丹波　越前　加賀　淡路

卆里拳

41. Nagakubo Sekisui: *Kaisei Nihon Yochirō Teizenzu* (Revised Map of All Japan and its Main Routes). Woodblock print, dated 1811, 83 × 134.5 cm, author's collection. This highly detailed map is a reprint of a map of 1779. The thorough legend at the lower left shows the marking system for provinces and dis-

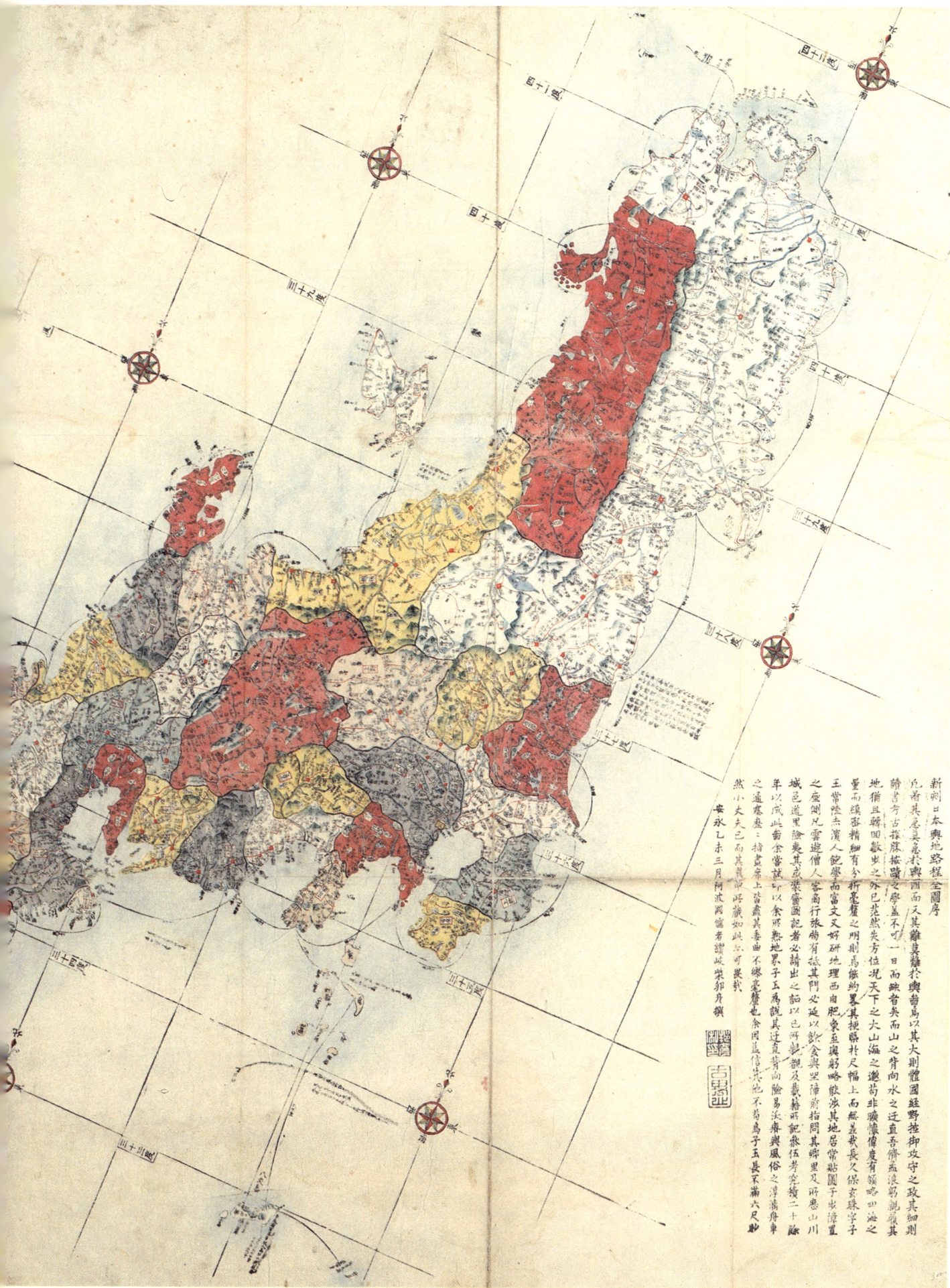

新刻日本輿地路程全圖序

凡畫其尾莫詭乎與番島以其大則體國延野控禦攻守之政其細則

謹按方古揖隊按蹟之學蓋不可一日而缺省與而山之背向水之迂直吾儕蓋浪郭就廣其

地猶且韓田散出之外已茫然失方位況天下之大山海之邈苟非職懷偉度有領略四海之

量而纖鄙精細有今析寛攫之明則焉能約畧其撮縣扶尺幅上而無盡載長久保玄珠字子

王常陸杰濱人飽學而富文友研地理西自肥象亞與郭畞欷沖其地居常粘圓于出讀置

之一座側九雲遊僧人客尚行承兩有誠其西門處延以飲食興之與里瀁指問年以成此衞宗嘗試已兩點圖記者必請出之詢以巳所山川

年以成此衞宗嘗試已兩點圖記者必請出之詢以巳所山川

之遙塞嚢一指盡帶上諮畞其委曲不緣寛攣也余固蓋信先地不苟爲子玉長某蒲六尺也

安永乙未三月阿波國儒者讃岐栄郃舟撰

然小丈夫乎而其即印听懷如此乞可覧狀

trics and their boundaries; routes; castle towns and military outposts; famous places, ancient castles and
battlegrounds; barriers; shrines and temples; and ports.

42. *Bankoku Sōzu* (World Map). Woodblock print, 1645, 58.8 × 136.6 cm, Kobe City Museum. The legends near the north and south polar regions are particularly interesting. The northern reads: "The people of this region live in daylight from the second to the eighth month and in darkness from the eighth to the second." The comment on the southern polar landmass frankly admits: "Since very few people have ever gone to these parts, we know nothing of the people or things there."

112

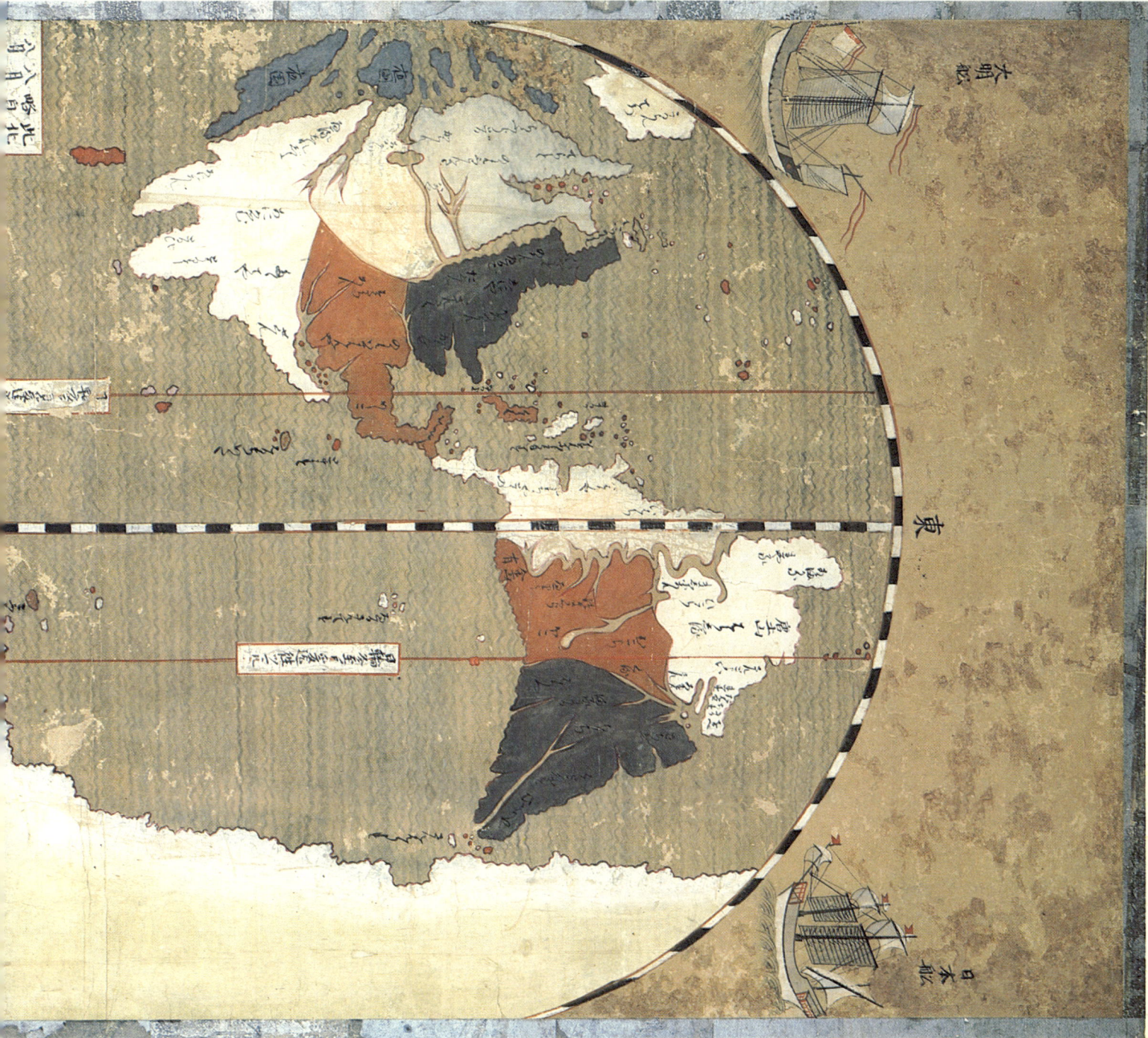

43. *Jimbutsuzu* (Pictures of Different Peoples). Woodblock print, 1645, 136.6×58.8 cm, Kobe City Museum. The print is mounted with the *Bankoku Sōzu* of the preceding plate. Cannibals (lower right), giants (lower left), and dwarves (column four, seventh from the top), share this scene with Europeans and Asians of many nations. A couple from Luzon, Philippines, is shown in the third column, second from the top. Above them are a Korean couple, and below them an Indian man and woman. The sixth and seventh scenes from the top in the same column feature English and Dutch couples.

44. Ishikawa Ryūsen: *Honchō Zukan Kōmoku* (Outline ▶ Map of Japan). Woodblock print, dated 1687, hand-colored, 59.9×139.8 cm, Kobe City Museum. In the lower left corner of this map Ishikawa acknowledges his debt to earlier Gyōgi-type maps, but points out the improvements he has made. He also lists the distances from Japan to various Chinese cities. Ezogashima intrudes at several places along the map's right border.

45. Inō Tadataka: map of western Japan. Manuscript, 1821, 203.5×162.1 cm, Kobe City Museum. Provinces are marked with red labels, and districts with yellow. Lines of latitude and longitude distinguish Inō's remarkably accurate map of southwestern Honshu, Shikoku, the Inland Sea, and Kyushu.

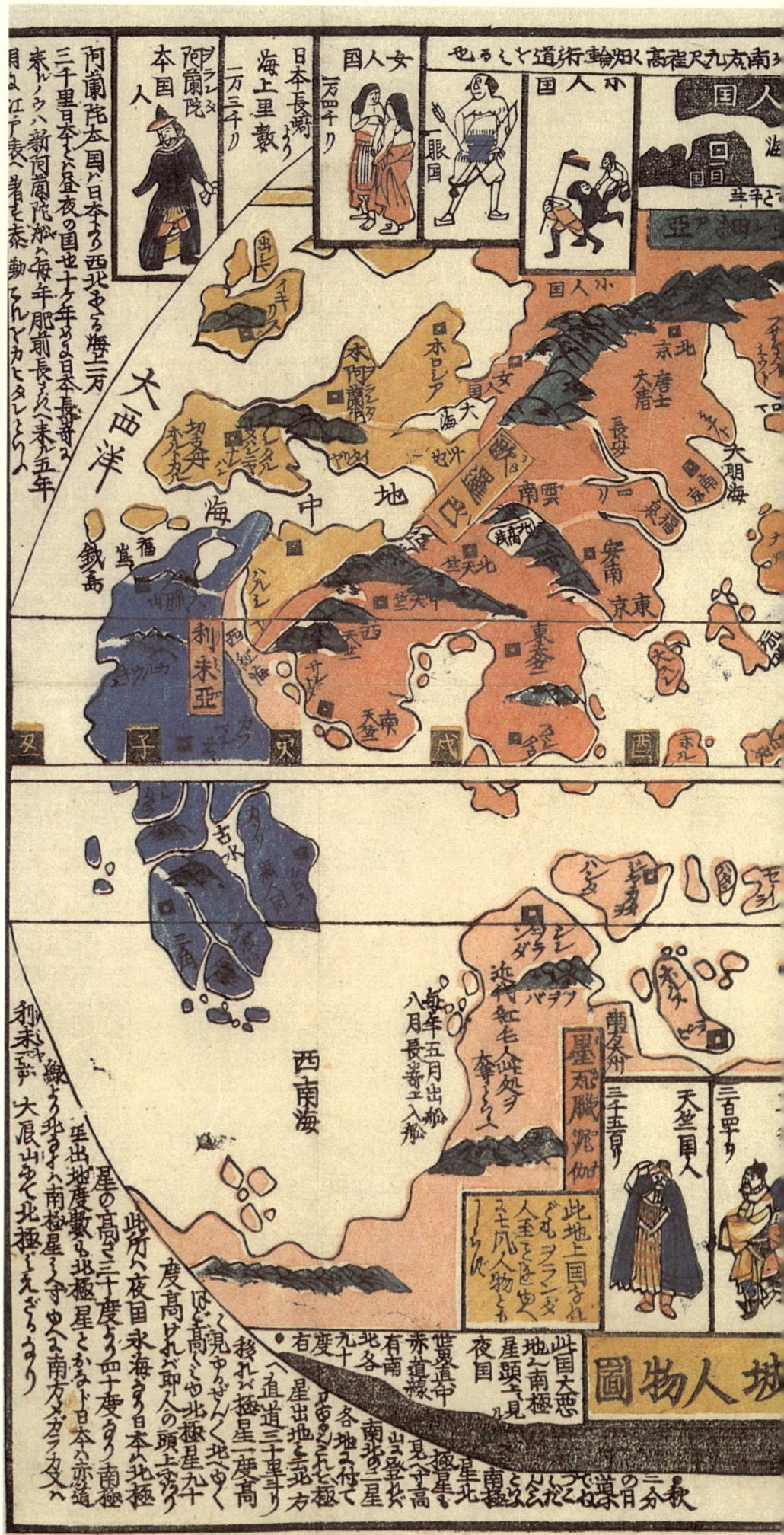

46. *Sekai Bankoku Yori Kaijō Risū Kokuin Ōjō Jimbutsuzu* (Map of the World Showing the Distances of Various Countries from Japan, Their Names, and Inhabitants of Their Capitals). Woodblock print, mid-nineteenth century, 34.9 × 48.3 cm, Kobe City Museum. This extremely inaccurate map is loosely based on that of Matteo Ricci. The inset figures are each accompanied by a short description of their country and its distance from Japan. There are several fanciful touches—giants, dwarves, cyclops, and, at the north pole, a "Land of the Night People." The steamships coursing to Japan from America are a herald of Perry's visit.

北アメリカ
人物

亞細亞 歐羅巴 亞利未亞
南北亞墨利加

大東洋

北亞墨利加

南亞墨利加

大日本大條州

タツタン國人

長人國

太南海

メガラ海

東南海

百峯

唐大唐人
南京
安南コウチ人

世界萬國日本ヨリ海上里数

北極星

南極星

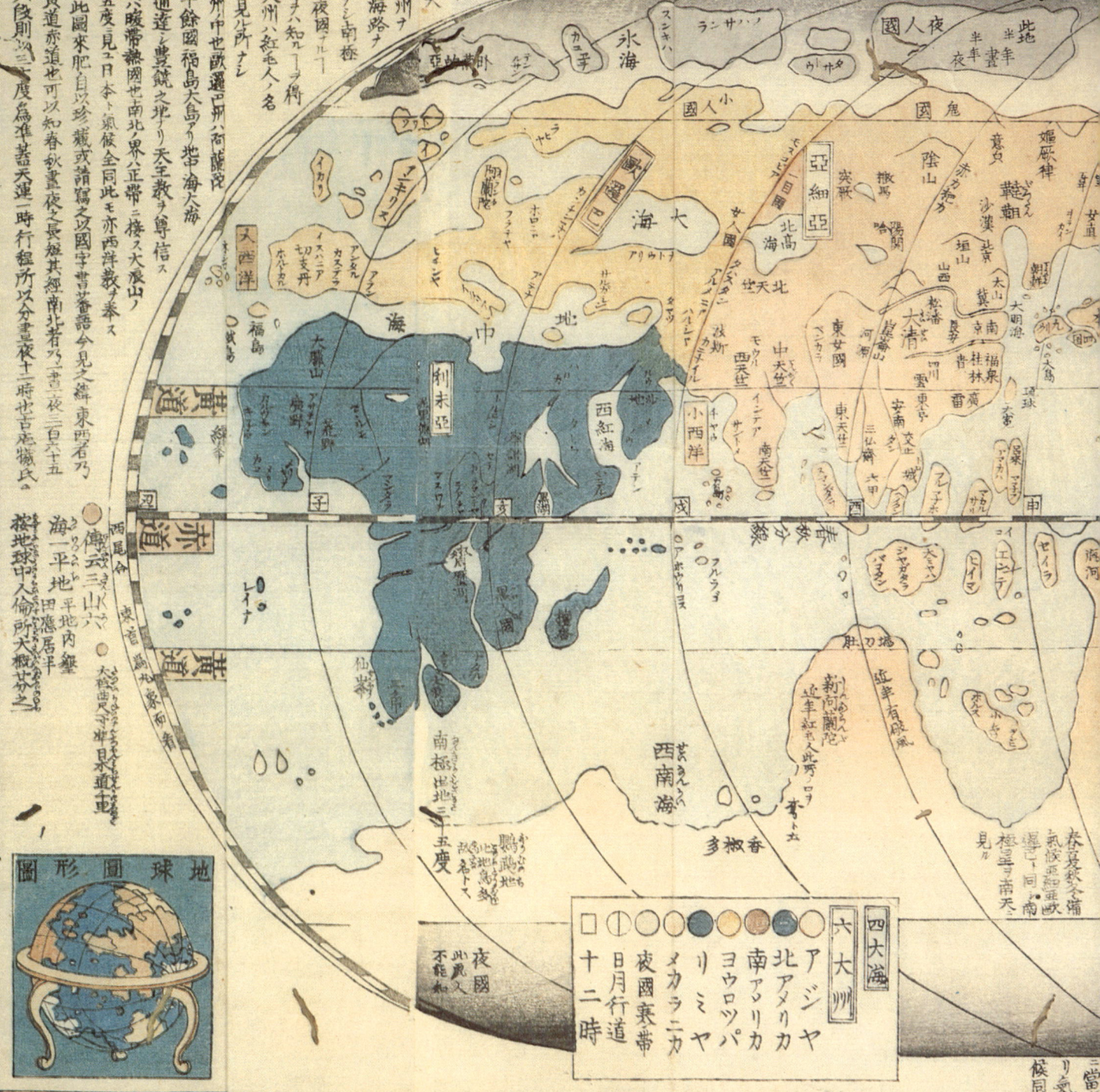

47. Abe Yasuyuki: *Bankoku Chikyū Yochi Zenzu* (Map of the World). Woodblock print, dated 1853, 36.8 ×65.2 cm, author's collection. This rather late map shows remarkably little improvement over its seventeenth-century predecessors.

萬國地球輿

安倍泰行卿撰著

北亞墨利加

南亞墨利加

氷海

夜人國

小東洋

大東洋

南海

東南海

赤道

銀島

銀河

珊瑚珠島

長人國

南方大州

48. Rōkashi: *Nansembushū Bankoku Shōka no Zu* (Buddhist Map of the World). Woodblock print, dated 1710, 118 × 145.2 cm, Kobe City Museum. A list of Buddhist sutras, Chinese histories, and other literary classics lies to the left of the title of this map. A land bridge connects China to an unnamed continent in the upper right corner, and the island of Ezo with its fief of Matsumae is located slightly to the south of the mystery continent.

49. *Nansembushūzu* (Buddhist Map of the World). Manuscript, early nineteenth century, 127.5 × 152.2 cm, Kobe City Museum. The airship at the top of this map is a delightful detail. Both this map and that in Plate 48 benefit from comparison to the *Gotenjikuzu* in Plate 11, the prototype from which they developed.

50. Map of Nagasaki. Woodblock print, dated 1680, 65 × 150 cm, British Library, London. This map was brought back to Europe by Engelbert Kaempfer, and shows Nagasaki harbor and ships with figures of foreigners. There is also a table of distances between Japan and various foreign countries, including Holland.

51. Jacques Nicholas Bellin: *Plan du Port de la Ville de Nangasaki*. Atlas leaf, 1763, Paris, 19.5 × 33.5 cm, author's collection. This map, which appears in volume three of the *Petit Atlas Francois* (5 volumes), offers an interesting comparison with Plate 50.

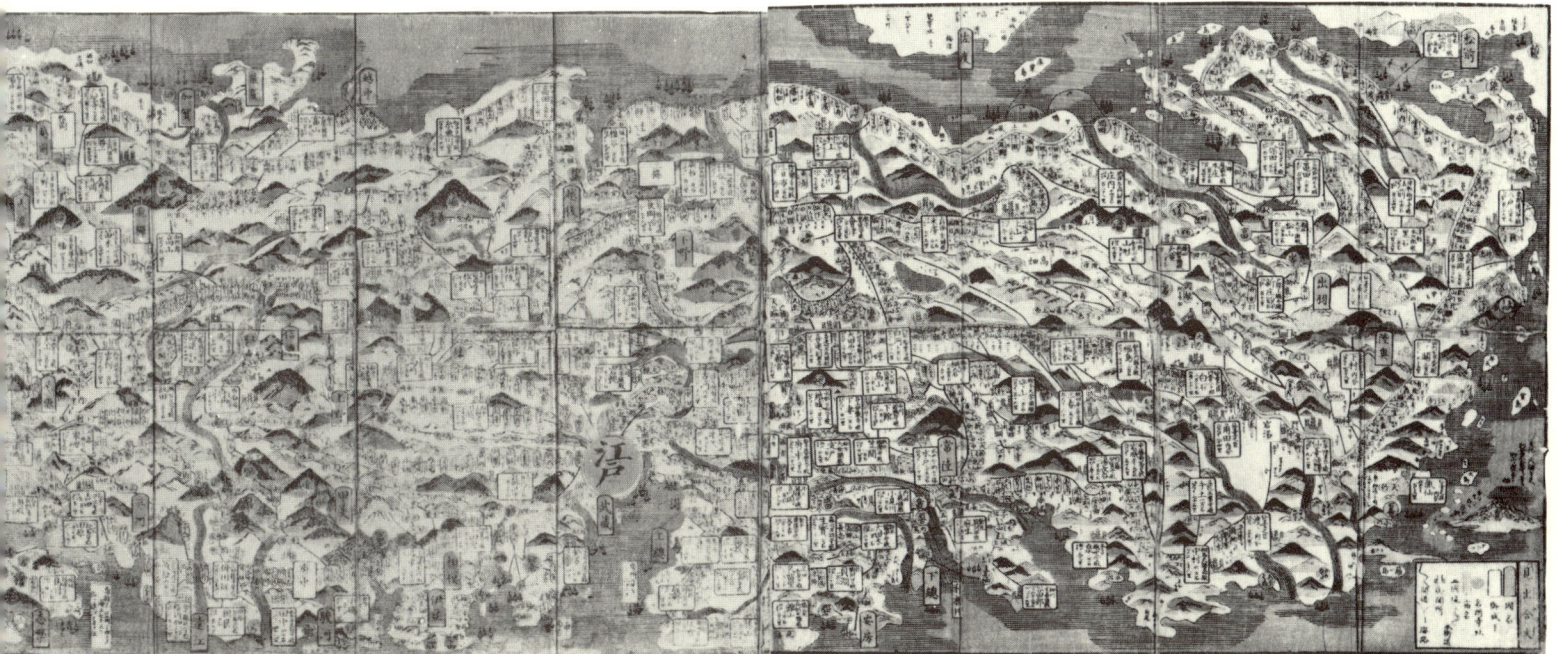

52. *Nihonkoku Dōchūzu* (Pictorial Route Map of Japan) Woodblock print, probably mid-nineteenth century, 35 × 175 cm, author's collection. See following page for a detail of the area surrounding the capital.

53. Detail, 35×34 cm, of *Nihonkoku Dōchūzu*, Plate 52. The large, centrally located red circle identifies Kyoto, with Lake Biwa to the right. Osaka and the Inland Sea can be seen in the lower left sector. This highly detailed route map shows not only the distance of each town from Edo, but also the number of *koku* for each fief.

125

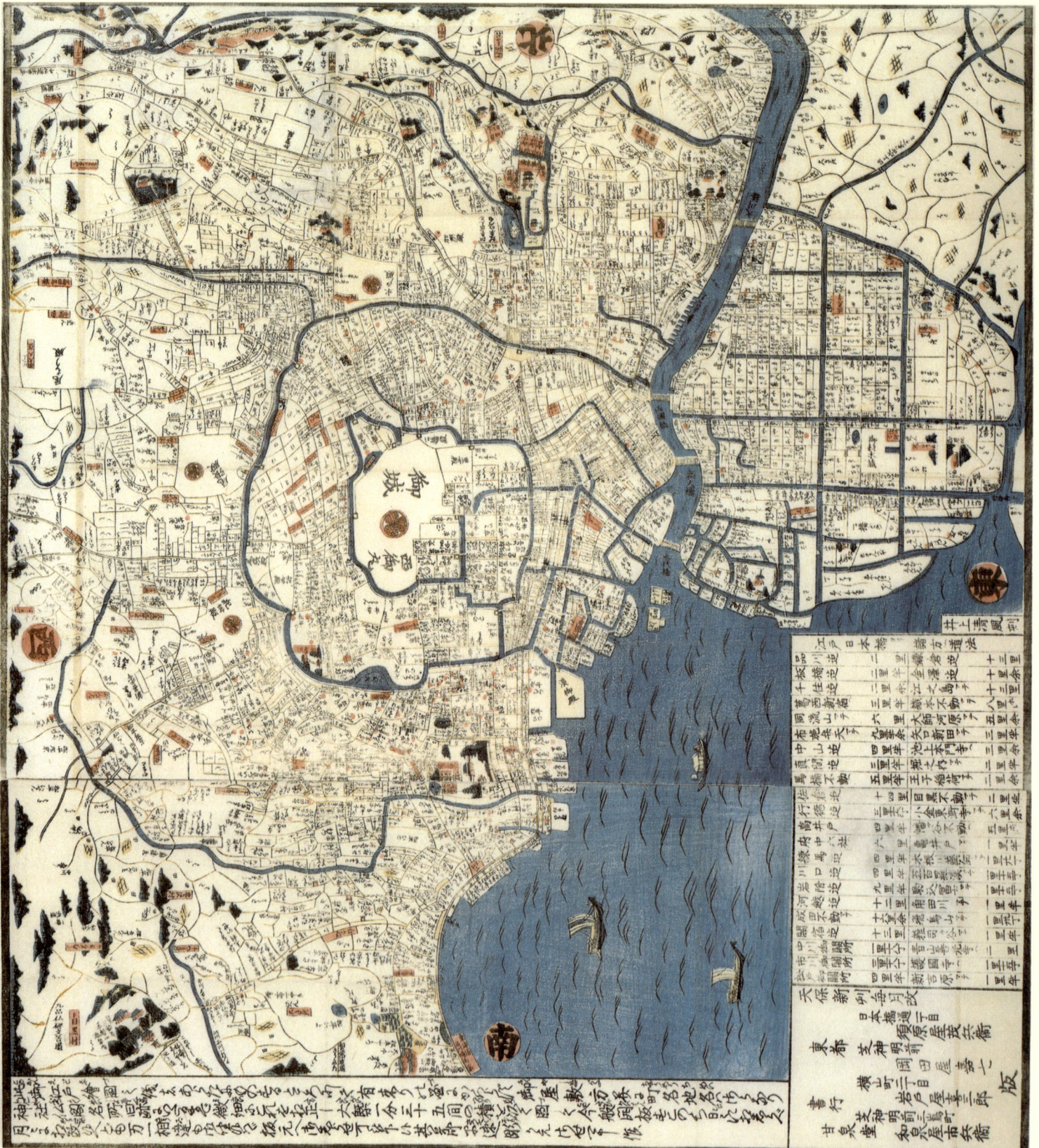

54. Map of Edo. Woodblock print, mid-nineteenth century, 57.8×47.2 cm, author's collection.
Described as being "revised monthly," this map of the Tempō era (1830–43) shows distances from Edo
to various places in Japan, and offers an interesting comparison with Plate 55.

126

55. J. van Schley: *Plan de Jedo*. Book leaf, 1752, Paris, 25 × 24.5 cm, author's collection. Though the general outline of Edo follows Japanese maps, Schley has exaggerated the size of Shinobazu Pond, greatly regularized the streets, byways, and even rivers, and seen fit to provide the imperial palace grounds with a formal, European-style garden. Schley's maps first appeared in Volume 10 of the *Histoire Generale des Voyages*, published from 1746 to 1789.

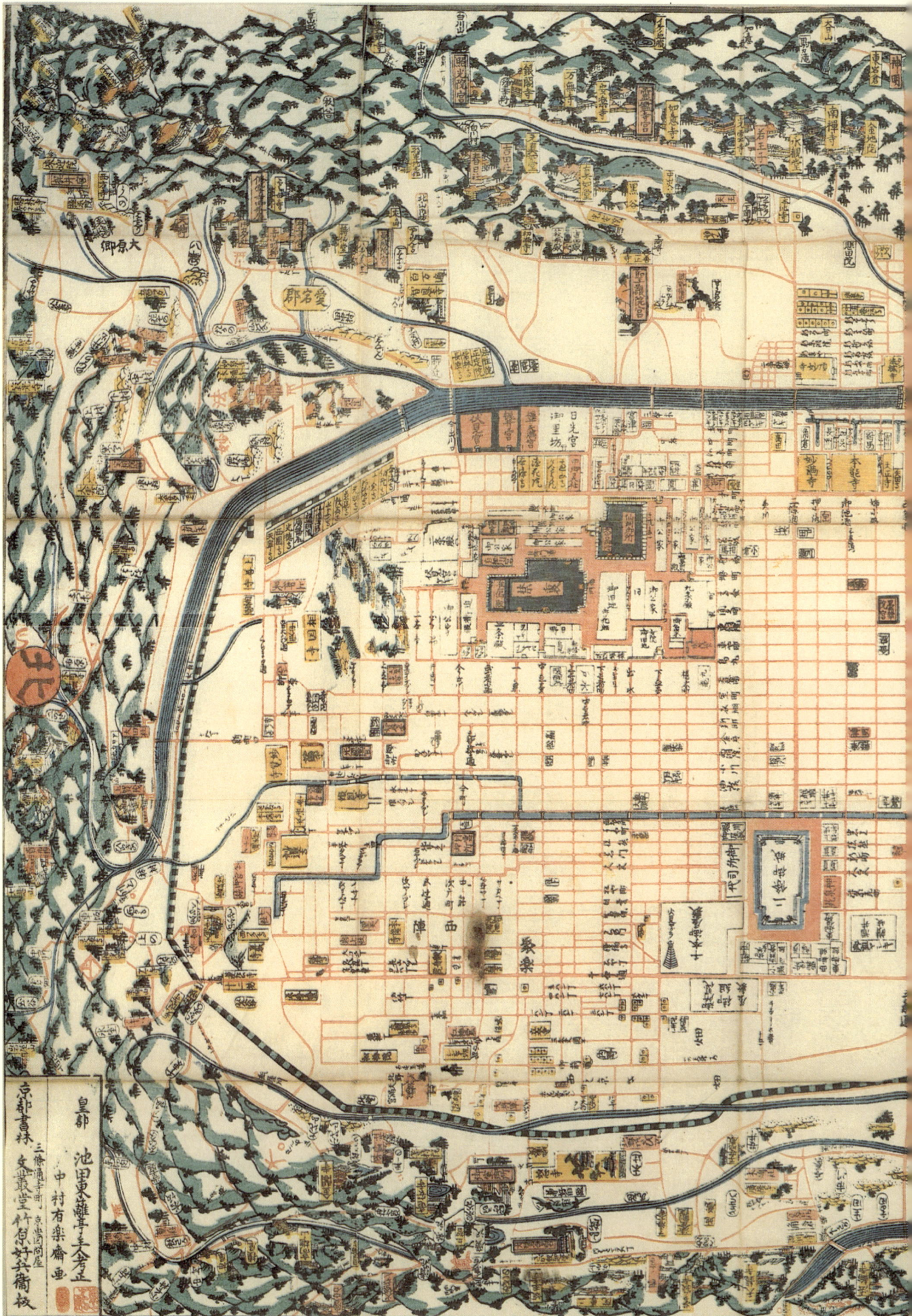

56. Takehara Yoshibei: map of Kyoto. Woodblock print, mid-nineteenth century, 69 × 102 cm, author's collection. The regular grid pattern of Kyoto's streets contrasts sharply with the layout of Edo. The east

(top) is dominated by the imposing Kiyomizu-dera temple. The yellow squares represent temples, the
pink squares shrines, and pink outlines in dark blue stand for imperial palaces and residences.

鎌倉繪圖

八幡宮

十二院

大佛

由比の濱

南

58. *Banchō Ezu* (Map of the Banchō Section of Edo). Woodblock print, dated 1852, 46.5×53.5 cm, author's collection. This printed map covers the area between Hanzōmon and Yotsuya in the south over to Ichigaya, and includes, to the north, the area that is now part of Yasukuni Shrine. Green areas represent imperial holdings.

◀ 57. *Kamakura Ezu* (Map of Kamakura). Woodblock print, mid-nineteenth century, 61.5×44.5 cm, author's collection. The Hachiman-gu shrine complex fills the upper portion of this map, which is bordered on the south by the sea. The great Buddha is visible in the southwest sector.

59. Katsushika Hokusai: *Tōkaidō Meisho Ichiran* (Panoramic View of Famous Places on the Tōkaidō Highway). Woodblock print, mid-nineteenth century, 35.2×122.3 cm, Kobe City Museum. Mt. Fuji rises majestically on the left side of this print. The old capital of Kyoto is located in the upper right corner,

it's grid-pattern streets clearly visible, while Edo is in the lower right. The bridge projecting out toward the viewer leads from Nihombashi to Shinagawa, according to the caption.

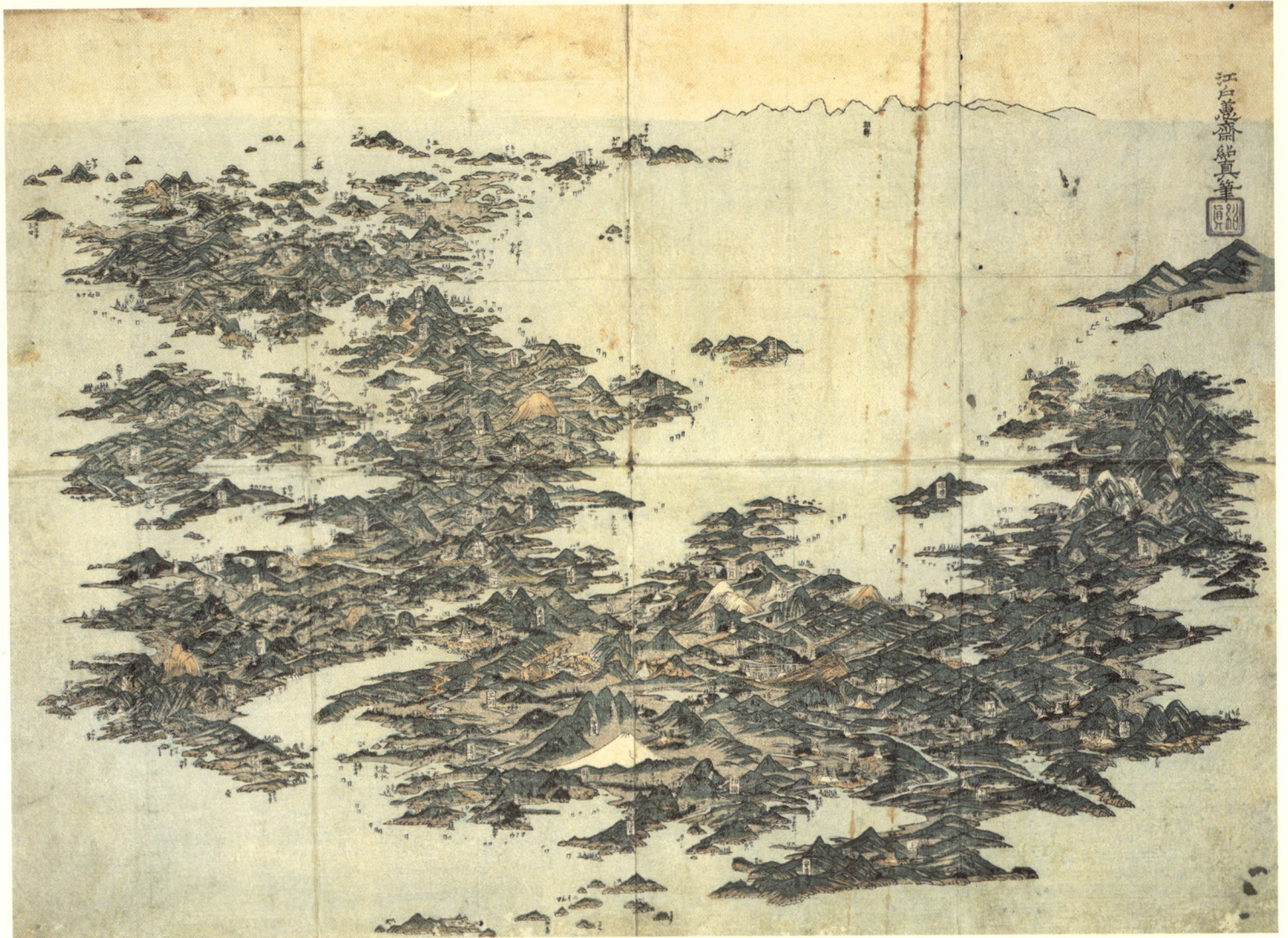

60. Kuwagata Keisai: *Nihon Ezu* (Bird's-eye View of Japan). Woodblock print, early nineteenth century, 39.8 × 57.4 cm, Kobe City Museum. *See also* insert inside back cover.

61. See following foldout ▶

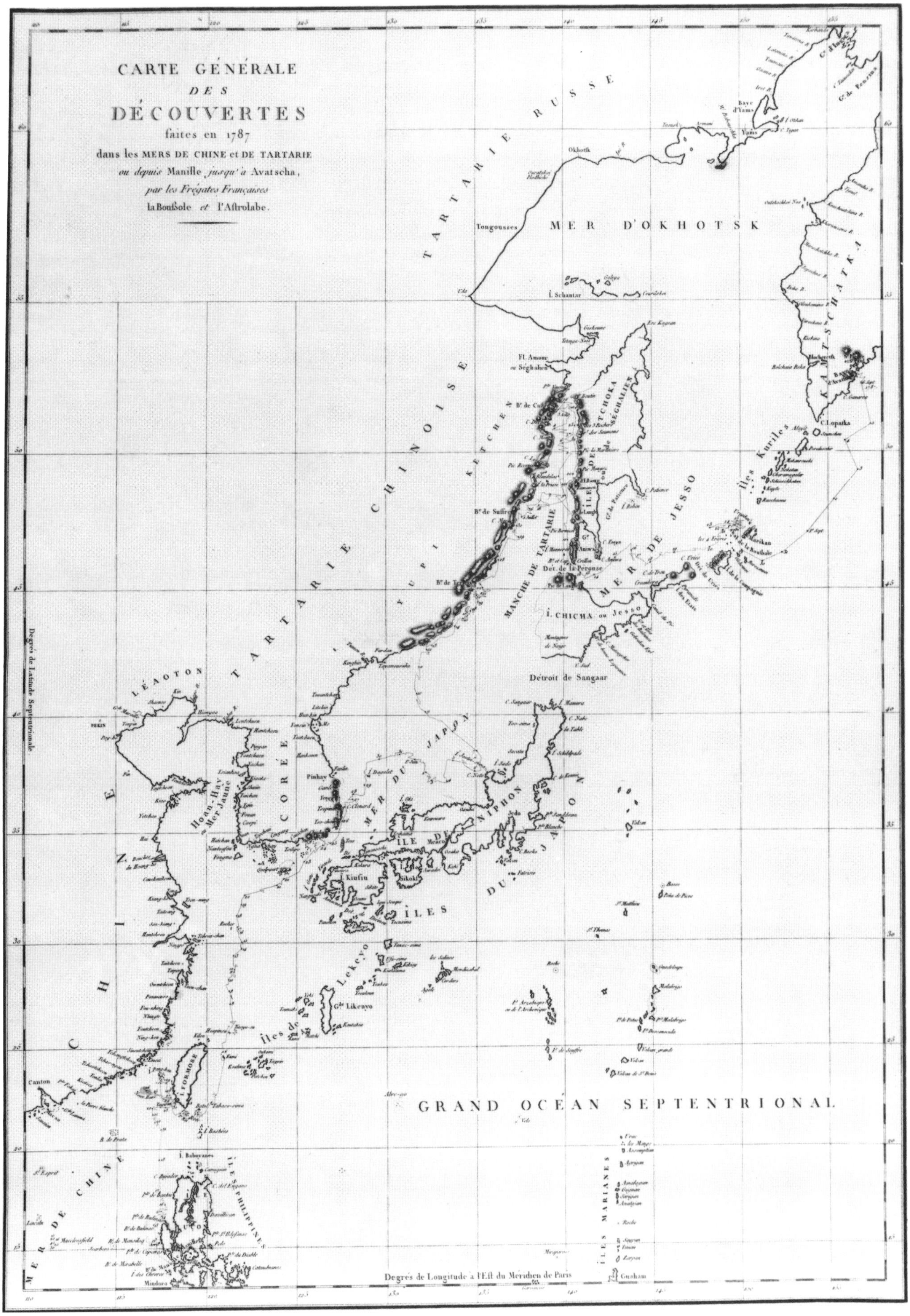

CARTE GÉNÉRALE

DES

DÉCOUVERTES

faites en 1787

dans les MERS DE CHINE et DE TARTARIE

ou depuis Manille jusqu'à Avatscha,

par les Frégates Françaises

la Boussole *et* l'Astrolabe.

TARTARIE RUSSE

MER D'OKHOTSK

Tongousses

Okhotsk

Î. Schantar

KAMTSCHATKA

C. Lopatka

Îles Kuriles

TARTARIE CHINOISE

Fl. Amour ou Séghalien

ÎLE DE TCHOKA ou SÉGHALIEN

MANCHE DE TARTARIE

Dét. de la Pérouse

MER DE JESSO

i. CHICHA ou JESSO

Détroit de Sangaar

PÉKIN

CORÉE

LÉAOTON

Hoan-Hai ou Mer Jaune

MER DU JAPON

MER DU LOU

ÎLE DE NIPHON

ÎLE DE XIMO

Kiusiu

Sikoki

ÎLES DU JAPON

CHINE

ÎLES de Lékéyo

Lékéyo

G.de Likenyo

Canton

FORMOSE

MER DE CHINE

ÎLES PHILIPPINES

Mindoro

i. Babuyanes

GRAND OCÉAN SEPTENTRIONAL

ÎLES MARIANES

Guaham

Degrés de Latitude Septentrionale.

Degrés de Longitude à l'Est du Méridien de Paris

62. La Pérouse: *Carte General*. Atlas leaf, date uncertain, 68 × 49 cm, author's collection. Published in Paris, La Pérouse's map shows the discoveries made by the ships La Boussole and l'Astrolabe in their voyages of 1788.

135

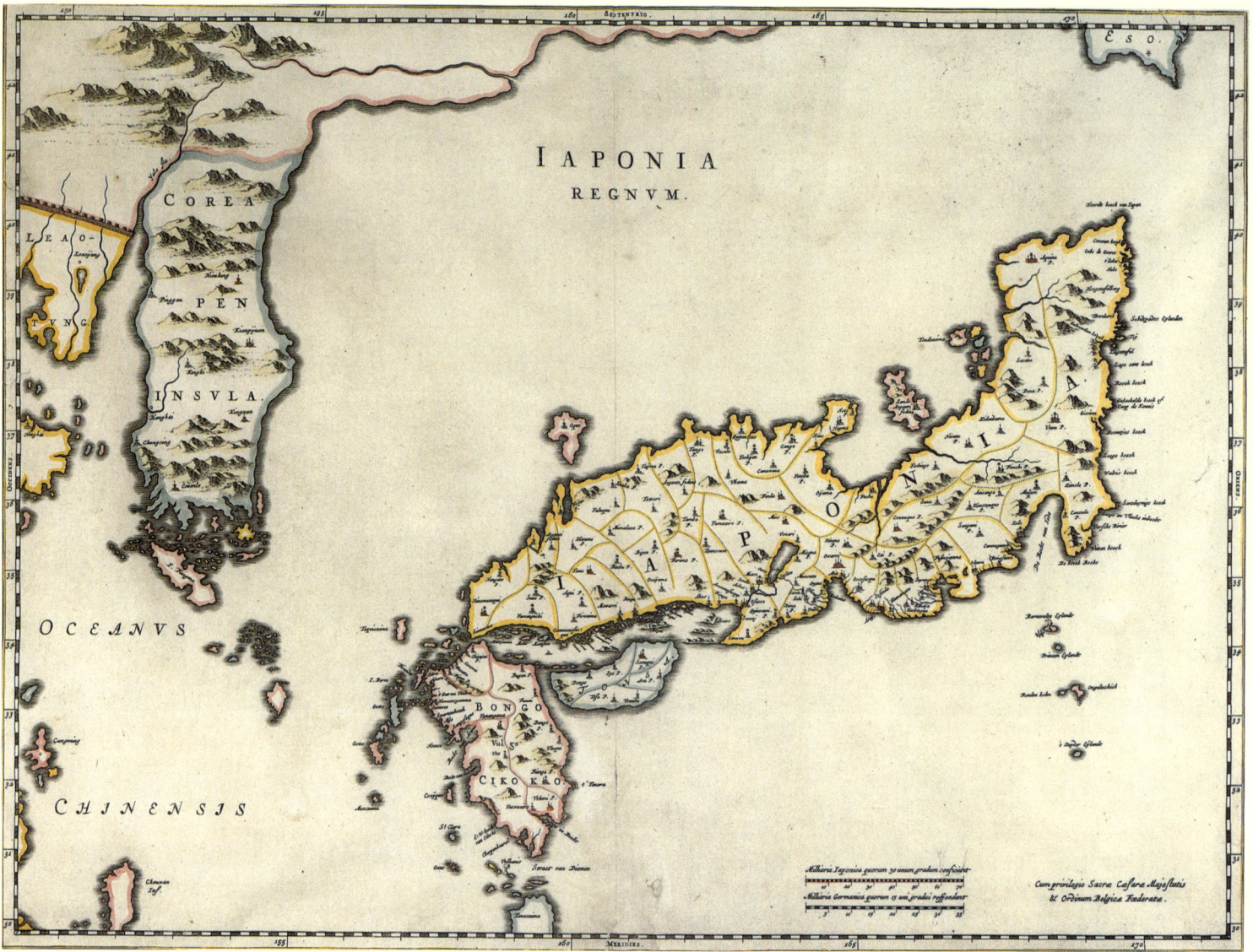

63. Martino Martini: *Iaponia Regnum*. Atlas leaf, 1655, 41.5 × 57 cm, author's collection. Martini's map was first published by Johann Blaeu in his *Atlas Sinensis* of 1655 in Amsterdam.

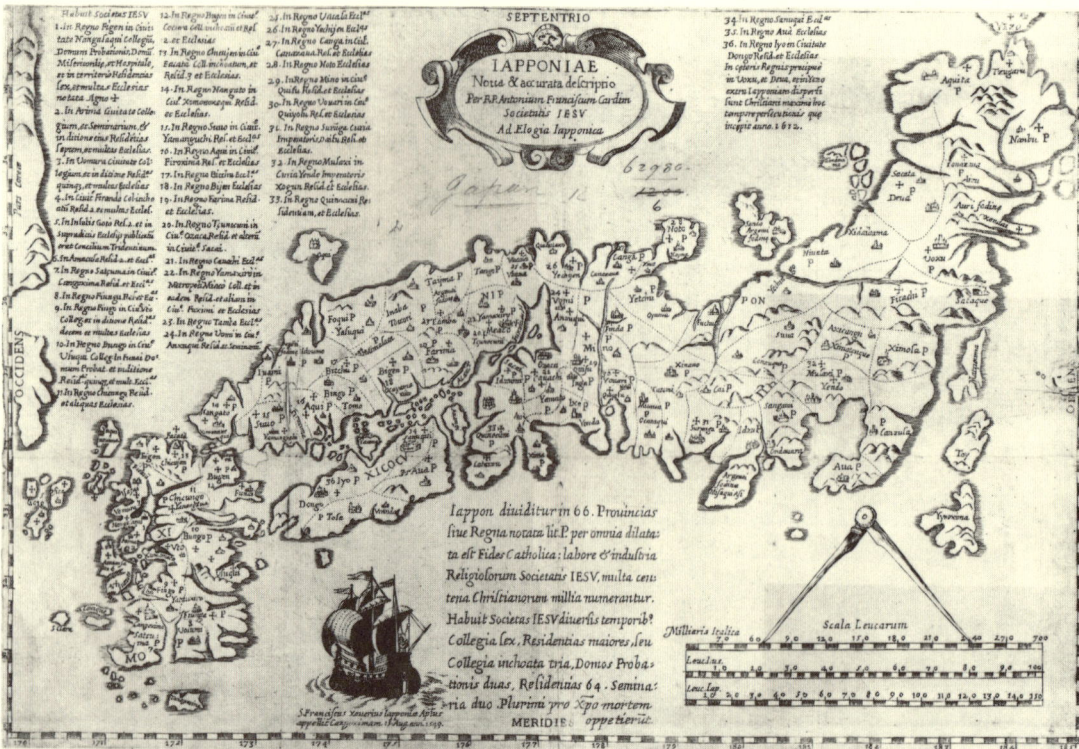

64. Antonio Cardim: *Iapponiae Nova & Accurata Descriptio*. Book leaf, 1646, Rome, 30.5 × 40.6 cm, British Library, London.

65. Robert Dudley: *Asia carta di ciasete piu moderna*. Book leaf, 1661, 42.5 × 55.5 cm, British Library, London. Dudley's map appeared in the *Arcano del Mare* published in Florence in 1661.

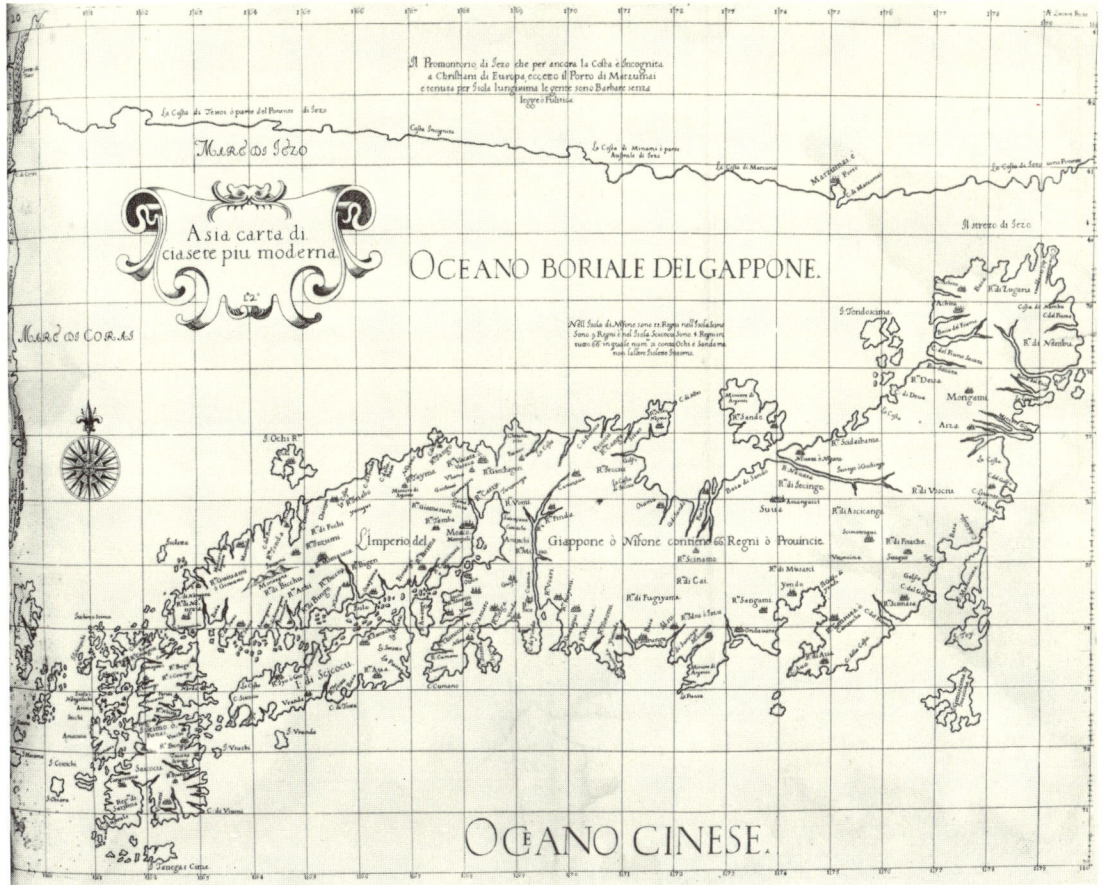

66. Robert Dudley: *Carta Particolare della Grande Isola de 'Giapone è di Iezo con il Regno di Corai et altre Isole in torno*. Book leaf, dated 1661, 48.5 × 75.5 cm, author's collection, print courtesy of Yūshōdō Booksellers. This map also appeared in the *Arcano del Mare*.

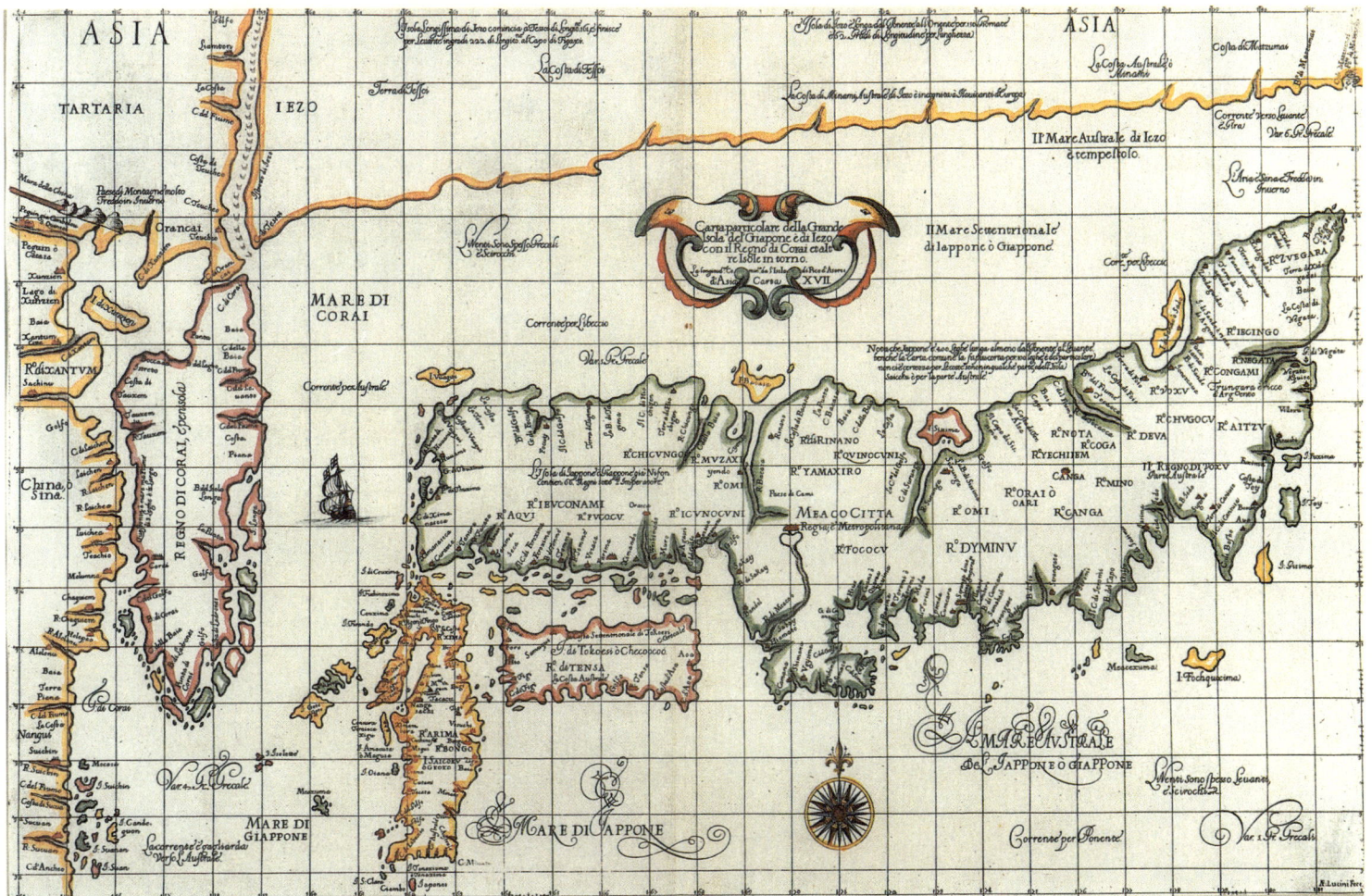

67. Phillipe Briet: *Royaume du Iapon*. Paris, ca. 1650, 37 × 52 cm, author's collection.

68. Nicolas Sanson: *Les Isles du Iapon*. Paris, 1683, 18.5 × 24 cm, author's collection. Sanson's map appeared under several slightly varying titles. This edition was published posthumously. The situation of Ezo is of note in this and the following two maps.

69. François Caron: *Perfeckte Kaert vande gelegentheydt des Landts van Iapan*. Book leaf, 1661, The Hague. 24.9 × 36.7 cm, Tenri Central Library, Nara. Here ''Iezzo'' is a land bridge connecting Japan to Tartary.

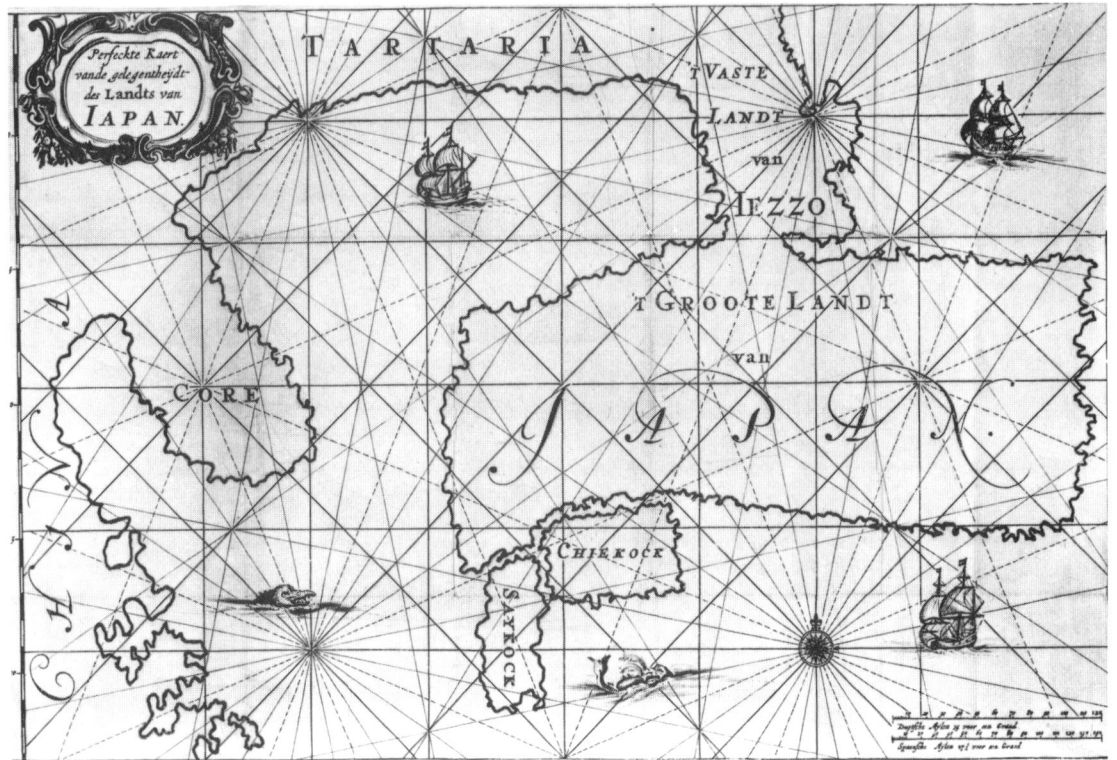

70. Jan Jansson: *Nova et Accurata Iaponiae Terrae Esonis ac Insularum adjacentium ex Novissima detectione descriptio Apud Ioannem Ianossonium*. Atlas leaf, 1659, Amsterdam, 55 × 45.5 cm, author's collection.

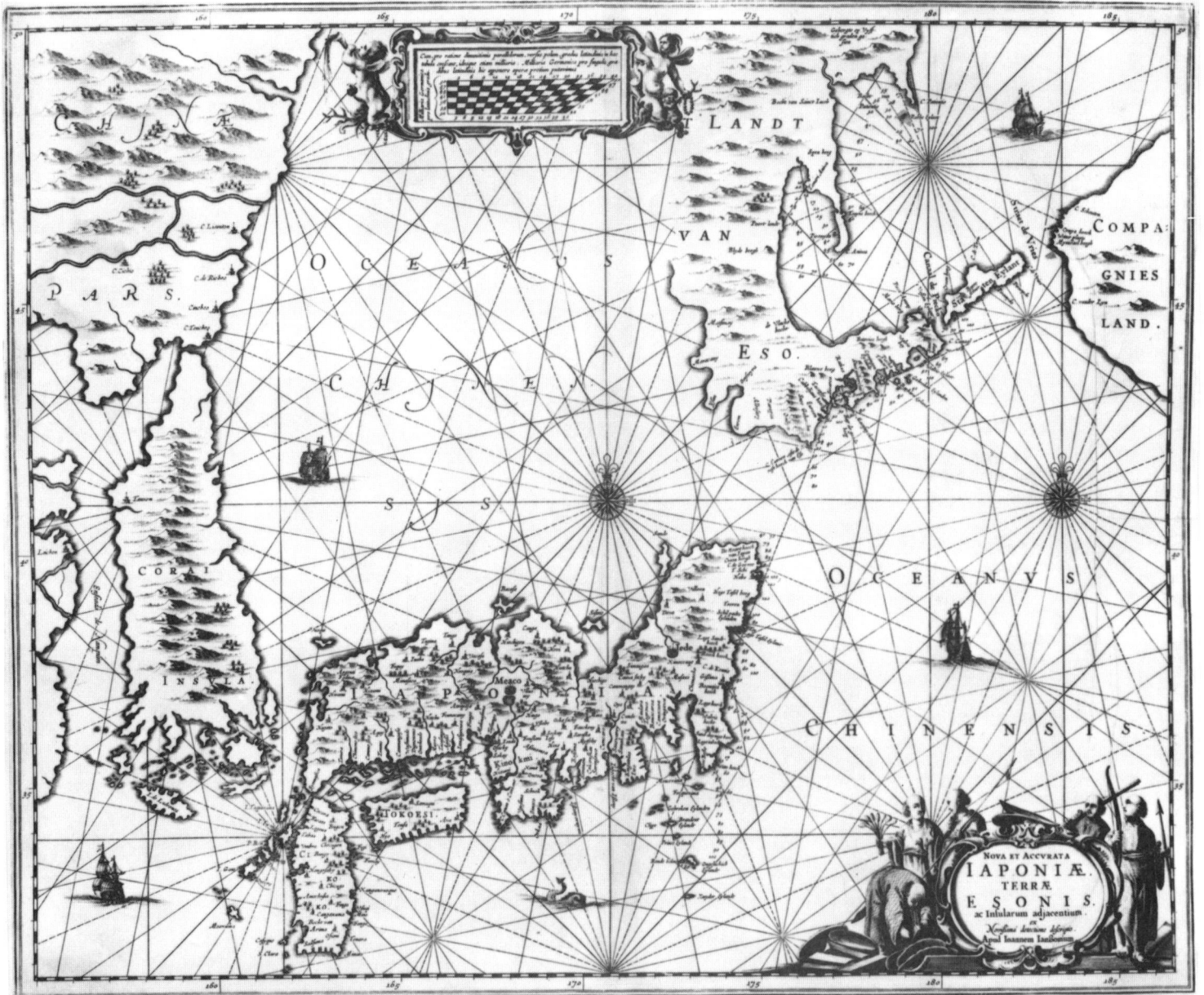

40

39

38

37

36

35

34

33

32

ISLE DE CORAY ou de COREER

CARTE DES ISLES DU

ESQUELLES EST REMARQVE' LA ROUTE TANT PAR MER QU

que tiennent les Hollandois pour se transporter de la Ville de Nangasaqui a IEDO *demeure du*

OCEAN ORIENTA

MER DE COREER

OQVI

Dans la prouince de Iamaisoit dans les montagnes, qui sont proche de la Ville de Inaba: C'est ou sont les mines les plus abondantes en argent

Quira Yecs noxo

Foovt INABA

Mines d'argent YAZVQVI

Vacosa VRAMA Vonr

IVAMI MIMALACA

TAVMA TANGO

TOTTORI

TAMBA YAMAXIRO

IAMAISOIT

IDZVMO BINGO BITCHV Tomo

BIGEN Tcinocvni FVXIMI

MIACO ou MEACO

Quasu

NANGATO SVVO Aqvi Oquayama Muro Farina Achas

Ingo

Ximonozoqui Firexima Iuto Sauia Singer Amanezima Wata Barima Auua

TOSACAN

SAGANIA

IDZVMI YAMATO Yxe

CAVACHI

Xoko

Sino Simo

Coysvima SANVQVI

ANAI

QVINOCVNI XIMA

L'Isle ou on enuoie la Ieunesse qui ne veut rien valoir et ou on les fait trauailler par force, iusque a ce que leurs plus prochai les en retire

Amatsima GinKey Coscong COCVRA

XIMO

Fvnay Bugen estoit la Demeure du prince qui se fit Chrestien auec deux de ses enfans

Xio IYO Dongo

TOKOESI ou XIKOKO Isle XIKOKO

AVA

IETSEN

Simizisima Iobeca Auwa

FIRANDO Ce lieu estoit autrefois la premiere demeure des Hollandois Les 3 Gotto

Sincubi Omoda Key Nanart gamma Zetta Rochei NANGASAQVI

LE ROYAUME DE SAIKOCK

Bungo

TOIA CATAIXU

Ximo, qui ort le lieu que tous les vaisseaux viennent reconnoitre auant que d'aborder la terre

Kisma Cest l'isle ou sont les Hollandois

Ximo SaiKock Satcuma

Vasumi Tanegaxima

CATAIXU

MER DU

71. Jean-Baptiste Tavernier : *Carte des Isles du Iapon*. Book leaf, 1679, Paris, 51.5 × 76.5 cm, author's collection.

140

APON
R TERRE
res mesmes Isles

TERRE DE
IESSO

Destroit
de Sangaar

TSVNGAER

AQVITA

NANBV

39

TONDO
XIMA
Isle

YONAZAVA

ATZN

38

Mines
d'argent SANDO

XENDAI

DEVA

Mines
d'or

VOXV

37

XIDAIBAMA

NIVATA

NObTO
NAYMA

FITAQVI

SATAQVE

YECHINGO

AXICANGA

XIVA
Canga

VRCHI

IVVA

O CHIOR

QVANTO

MACVAINA Isle

35

CONTQVE

AXIMOT
Caqui

XIMOLV

MVLAXI

XINANO

IEDO ou IENDO
demeure du Roy

TATOMI

SANGAMI

MICAVA

Fusino amma
montagne toujours
couuerte de
neige

CANTVLA

TOI Isle

34

DAFLA

ERI

AVA

BANDEL

Dans ceste prouince
de Bandel
il y a aussi des
mines d'argent

33

Ceste pointe est apellée
la pointe de Misaqui

YYNOXIMA Isle

Auec Priuilege du Roy

Lieues du Iapon ensemble
petites Lieues de France
5 10 15 20 25 30

Durant fecit.

72. Arnoldus Montanus: *Iedo*.
Book leaf, 1669, Amsterdam, 28 ×
77 cm, author's collection. In
Altas Japonnensis, English edition by
John Ogilby, 1670.

73. Arnoldus Montanus: *Osacco*.
Book leaf, 1669, Amsterdam, 26 ×
69 cm, author's collection. Plate
from the same work.

IEDO

OSACCO

SUCCESSION DES EMPEREURS DU JAPON AVEC UNE
RECEPTION DES AMBASSAD...

Meurtre de Cubo Empeur du Japon.

Explication de la Figure.

1. Mioxindono, devant lequel les Japonnois se prosternent. 2. Hutes des Soldats. 3. Chariets des Japonnois. 4. L'Empereur Cubo blessé à la poitrine. 5. Deux cens Gentils-hommes Japonnois. 6. Tour Jmperiale. 7. Corps de Garde des Soldats, à la porte de la Ville. 8. Muraille de la Ville. 9. Soldats qui escaladent la muraille. 10. Peuples du Japon qui descendent de la montagne.

Histoire de Meurtre de Cubo.

Cubo etoit un des Principaux Rois du Japon, chez qui l'Imperatrice femme du premier Dayro, se refugia, pour lui demander du secours contre les Rebelles qui avoient detrôné l'Empereur son Epoux. Ce Roi l'aiant reçu avec de grans temoignages de respect, s'offrit d'employer sa Couronne & sa vie pour mettre sur le Trône le veritable Successeur du Dayro. Il mit en effet une puissante armée sur pié, & aiant vaincu & fait prisonnier le rebelle Oxima, il lui ôta la vie par une mort cruelle. Cubo pour recompense de ce service, fut fait General de l'Empire. Il ne fut pas longtems fidele au nouvel Empereur: Comme l'Imperatrice Mère gouvernoit plus que son fils & ne songeoit qu'à ses plaisirs, Cubo ne put longtems souffrir la domination d'une femme qui lui devoit l'Empire; il commença à le brouiller avec son fils, & d'en venir ensuite à la force ouverte pour se mettre lui même sur le Trône. Il entreprit une guerre cruelle, qui dura six ans. Il se fit durant ce tems-là un grand carnage; & Cubo r'aiant ajoûté une nouvelle victoire sur les troupes de l'Imperatrice, cette Princesse en mourut de regret. Le faible Empereur fit la paix avec Cubo, aux depens de sa propre Couronne.

Les choses demeurérent en cet état durant 5, ou 6 autres années, que Cubo jouit paisiblement du Trône. Mais Mioxindono, qu'il avoit fait son General, resolut enfin de le detrôner, comme il avoit detrôné lui-même le Dayro. Cubo avoit pour femme Mirima, qui etoit d'une rare beauté. Mioxindono, qui avoit occasion de la voir souvent, en devint amoureux & s'en fit aussi aimer. Mais au bout de quelque tems, cette Princesse etant entrée par devotion dans un Monastere de Bonzes, Maison Royale, dont tous les Religieux etoient gens de qualité, & aiant vu le neveu du Superieur, nommé Omendono, qui etoit le plus beau garçon du Monde, âgé, seulement de 18 à 19 ans, elle ne put deffendre son cœur de l'aimer avec violence. Mioxindono s'aperçut de quelque refroidissement de la part de sa Maitresse: il en chercha la cause, & l'aiant bientôt decouverte, par la penetration ordinaire aux amans jaloux, Il surprit la Princesse dans le Monastere avec son nouveau Galant; Il immola celui-ci à sa vengeance, & blessa l'Imperatrice dangereusement. L'Empereur resolut venger l'insolence de son General, mais celui-ci qui avoit entre les mains les forces de l'Empire, assiegea Cubo dans sa Capitale, entra de vive force, y mit le feu aux quatre coins & fit perir ce malheureux Empereur de la maniere representée ci dessus.

Carte du JAPON.

(side genealogy panel, partly legible):
CAMIO SAMA se fils regna 1610.

DAIFU MA Tuteur Fandasyori le detrôna en...

Prince age de ... ans, fils de Nabunanga, en 15... tous à l'Idole de Foxis...

AXIM fils aîné de Da... se revolta contre ... & ... fut ... mor...

CUBO 1. usurpateur regna apres Dayro en 1551.

74. Henri Abraham Chatelain: *Carte du Japon*, plus two illustrations: *Meutre du Cubo Empereur du Japon* and *Reception des Ambassadeurs Hollandois au Japon*. Book leaf, 1719, Amsterdam, 11.5×15.5 cm. (map), author's collection. Chatelain produced two maps of Japan in 1719, one along the lines of Adrian Reland (see Pl. 77) and this map, which is a variant of the Teixeira map of 1595 (see Pl. 26). The two illustrations and the explanatory texts in French are based on Montanus's work. (see Pls. 72 and 73). The story under the left view and the genealogy of the rulers of Japan in the middle have little relationship to actual historical events.

144

Reception des Ambassadeurs Hollandois au Japon

Explication de la Figure

1 Ambassadeurs Hollandois. 2 Gouverneur de la Ville.
3 Suite des Ambassadeurs. 4 Trompettes des Vaisseaux Hollandois
5 Suite du Gouverneur. 6 Interprète. 7 Joueurs d'instrument.
8 Porteurs de chaise. 9 Cavalerie. 10 La Mer. 11 Le Quai.

Ambassade des Hollandois au Japon

Ce fut en l'année 1644 que Mr. Blekhovius aiant été choisi avec ses Collegues par messieurs de la Compagnie de Batavia pour la Celebre Ambassade du Japon, se rendit à Jedo, où il obtint son audience le 7. d'Avril. Les Ambassadeurs commencerent cette ceremonie par le bain qu'ils prirent la Veille, n'étant pas permis de se présenter devant l'Empereur sans s'etre baigné auparavant. L'Empereur s'étant trouvé indisposé le jour marqué pour l'audiènce ils parurent devant le Prince son fils, qui les reçut accompagné de tous ses Ministres. Ils furent conduits au Palais Royal avec leur suite qui étoit très nombreuse & très magnifique. Ils entrerent d'abord dans une Grande Sale, dont la moitié du Plancher étoit couverte de ces belles nates fines qui se font en ce pays là: le reste vernissé de cet admirable vernis qu'on ne peut imiter ailleurs qu'au Japon. La Garde de cette Sale n'étoit composée que de Seigneurs de la premiere qualité. De là ils passerent par plusieurs Chambres, toutes richement meublées, & où on les fit attendre près d'une heure & demie. Aubout de ce tems-là, ils furent introduits devant le fils de l'Empereur & devant ses Ministres, a qui ils firent leurs presens. Le sujet de cette Ambassade, fut de rendre graces à S.M. Japonnoise de celle qu'il avoit faite aux Hollandois prisonniers en les remettant en liberté, & de lui demander la continuation de son amitié, & la permission de Negocier dans son Empire. Entre les instructions qui furent données au Chef de cette Ambassade il lui étoit sur tout recommandé de retrancher de ses discours toutes les paroles superflues, & d'apuyer la moderation qu'il feroit paroitre en toutes choses sur la qualité de Marchand, qui ne permet pas à ceux de cette Profession de vaquer aux affaires d'état pour marquer qu'en agissant dans cette Ambassade que du Commerce de la Compagnie, il faloit eviter de donner de la jalousie aux Japonnois & de leur faire soupçonner qu'on pût rien entreprendre contre leur Empire, d'autant plus que la vanité aiant ruiné jusqu'alors les affaires de la Compagnie, on ne pouvoit les retablir que par beaucoup de modestie, & d'attachement à maintenir ses interêts. Les Ambassadeurs furent encore chargez de se comporter en tout avec frugalité & retenue, de n'avoir point de tables ouvertes & d'eviter la trop grande frequentation des Japonnois.

145

Miglia d'Italia

Leghe di Francia

Leghe di Spagna

Leghe d'Alemagna

Leghe communi di Mare

Stadi Chinesi

COREA et NIOCENCOUL

CHINA

Questa Penisola di Corea,
che da alcuni si crede
Isola, viene chiamato
Caregi, Niocencouk, e Caoli.

O C

Isola

Hoian

Tunglou

Saawan

Vatu Mont

Tatuno fl

Pinggan

Peyo Monti
KINGKI

NIENKIN

Hienkino

Hanchu

KINGAN, ò

CUNCHING, ò

Kinnan, ò
Yinhan

MAHAN YINHAN
Hoang Mont
Chuncug

CHUENLO, ò

Cuenlo
PIENHAN

COREIO

DELLA

Questo Nauilio, e usitato dalli Giaponesi, da loro ch...
Tayona, ch' ordinariamente hà 20 remi per parte, e...
in forma d'Elefante, et alla Poppa hà uno specchio assai g...
con una Camera, e Timane alla Portughese, quale u...
con tanta celerita, ch' in giorni 12. uà da Osacca...
sacqui, che sono in distanza di 220 Leghe di F...
cia per mare

Nangato

MARE

ITHAUGMA

ISOLA
TEQUICIIMA

FIRANDO

A. Toyen
B. Goetric
C. Comilla
D. Casarissima
E. Isle Cakessima
F. Klismor de hoogebon
G. Wikitsima

ISOLE
DELOTTO

Canal, le Goods
Tapuceumo

Sinnasco

NANGASACHI

Ste Claire

Oena

ME P. Tramontana

Maestro

Ponente

Garbino

Ostro

Scirocco Or

Levante

ORIEN

75. Vincenzo Maria Coronelli: *Isola del Giapone e Peninsola di Corea*. Dated 1692, Venice, 45.5×61 cm, author's collection. Ezo has been named Tartaria de Yupi, and is connected to the mainland in Coronelli's map.

146

ISOLA DEL GIAPONE
e
PENISOLA DI COREA
Dedicata
AL MOLTO REV.DO P.RE FONTAINE
della Compagnia di Gesù Assistente di Francia
dal P.M. CORONELLI M.C. COSMOGRAFO della SERN.MA
REPVBLICA DI VENETIA

Matsmay, è Città capitale de Yupi, e
seggio del loro Governatore Trafica
no castoro colli Giapponesi di Pelli pre
ciose, di Piume, ed Vecelli Gli Ha-
bitattori uestono alla Giapponese,
uiuono di legumi d'ogni sorte
abbondano di Pesci, Lardo
e d'Oglio di Balena,
di cui parimente
si nodriscono.

Settentrion

TARTARIA
DE
YUPI

Sinnandone, ò
Matsumay, e
Matsmay

STRETTO DE ZUNGAR
ò
SANGAR

O C E A N O

SANDO ISOLA

Tondo xima

MARE DEL GIAPONE

Gebroocke Eylanden, ò
Isola Rotta

Vulcan

Isola de
Barneuelts

Isola del
Prencipe

Onseluckick, ò
Malheureus

Romden holm
Baia Ratonda

MARE AUSTRALE

DE DIEMEN

si uende presso Domenico Padoani
sul ponte di Rialto all'Insegna
della Geografia

Mezo di Giorno

Oriente

Tab. VIII.   IMPERIVM JA
Ex ipsorum Japonensium mappis

76. Engelbert Kaempfer: *Imperium Iaponicum in sexaginta et octo Provincias divisum*. Book leaf, 1727, London, 46×53 cm, author's collection. Kaempfer's map, notable for its rather idiosyncratic attempts at duplicating Chinese characters, appears in his *History of Japan*. The inset at the lower left shows the rosaries of various Buddhist sects, and the gods of good luck—Ebisu holding a *tai* (sea bream)—decorate the lower border. Insets at the upper right are details of the northern territories.

148

NICVM IN SEXAGINTA ET OCTO PROVINCIAS DIVISVM.
servationibus Kæmpferianis, qua fieri licuit fide & cura descriptum a JOH CASPARO SCHEVCHZER
Tigurino, e Regia Societate et Collegio Medico Londinensi.

JESOGASIMA
longa, ut ferunt
300 Milliaria
Meacensia

Insulæ Septentrionalia, et Jesogasima
dionalia Littora, velut delineata extant
in qua reditus Provinciarum, Principum
fectorum nomina curiose exponantur.

J E S O
G A
S I M A

O S V
N I A E

Nautica Pyxis apud Sinas et Japones, prius
quam Europæis nota, usu percelebris.

Japonici Imperij à variis Terrarum Orbis partibus distantiæ
juxta Japones & eorum milliaribus.

A Japonia ad Tiusan	330	A. Jap. ad Bakksju	630	A Jap ad Tunkin	1600
Nankin	340	Sakasaggo	640	Tsiampan	1070
Nesa	340	Kimmon	640	Kabotsja	1800
Unsju	360	Kammon	660	Tani	2200
Taisju	370	Ankai	670	Rokkon	2400
Saksju	430	Tsieoau	800	Siam	2400
Pokin	480	Kesseki	800	Tuusu	2400
Fuxusju	510	Canto	880	Diagatara	3300
Senssju	570	Cannan	1480	Oranda	13200

MAT SVMAI

DO SA SI

NOTO

KA GA

JEETSIV

JETSINGO

Z OSIV

DEWA

OKI. I.

JDSV MI

FOOKI

TA SIMA

TAN GO

IMABA

UMASAKA

BITSIV

BINGO

BIDSEN

FARIMA

N G

JAMASII RO

JETSISSEN FIDA

KOOD SVKE MOODSVKE

FITATS

SI NA NO

KAI

MVSASI
Jedo, Sedes

SIMOOSA

OOMI

MINO

OWARI

MI KA WA

SVRVNGA

SANGAMI

KADSVSA

IGA

ISI E

TOO TOMI

IDSV

A WA

SIKOKF

AWADSI

KAWA TSII

JAMAT

NAI

IDSVMI

SSIMA

KII NOKVNI

VGO

IV

Nautica Pyxis Japonum

Viro Perillustri
Dno HANS SLOANE, Baronetto,
Collegii Medicorum Londinensis, et Societatis
Regiæ Præsidi, Copiarum Brittanicarum
Archiatro, Regiæ Scientiarum Academiæ
Parisiensis Sodali, &c.
Hanc Japonici Imperij Tabulam,
In grati animi monumentum,
Cum ob maxima ab ipso in me collata beneficia,
tum quod Res Japonicas suo Museo asservatas
ad illustrandam Japonum Historiam benevole
communicaverit,
Lubens meritoque sacram esse voluit J.C. SCHEVCHZER

Tofsitoku Fortunæ Deus,
apud Japones.

Daikoku
Divitiarum
Deus.

149

77. Adrien Reland: *Imperium Japonicum*. Atlas leaf, 1715, Amsterdam, 46 × 59.5 cm, author's collection. Adrien Reland's map was widely copied in the eighteenth century, even though it was not as accurate as earlier maps. Reland, a scholor, relied on Japanese sources and never actually visited Japan.

78. Mattheus Seutter: *Imperium Japonicum*. Atlas leaf, 1745, Augsburg, 57.5×46.5 cm, author's collection. Seutter's map is closely copied from Reland's, with minor decorative changes.

79. Pieter van der Aa: *William Adams Reystogt na Oost Indien*, Book leaf, 1707, Leyden, 23×15 cm, author's collection. The cartouche shows William Adams in the East Indies.

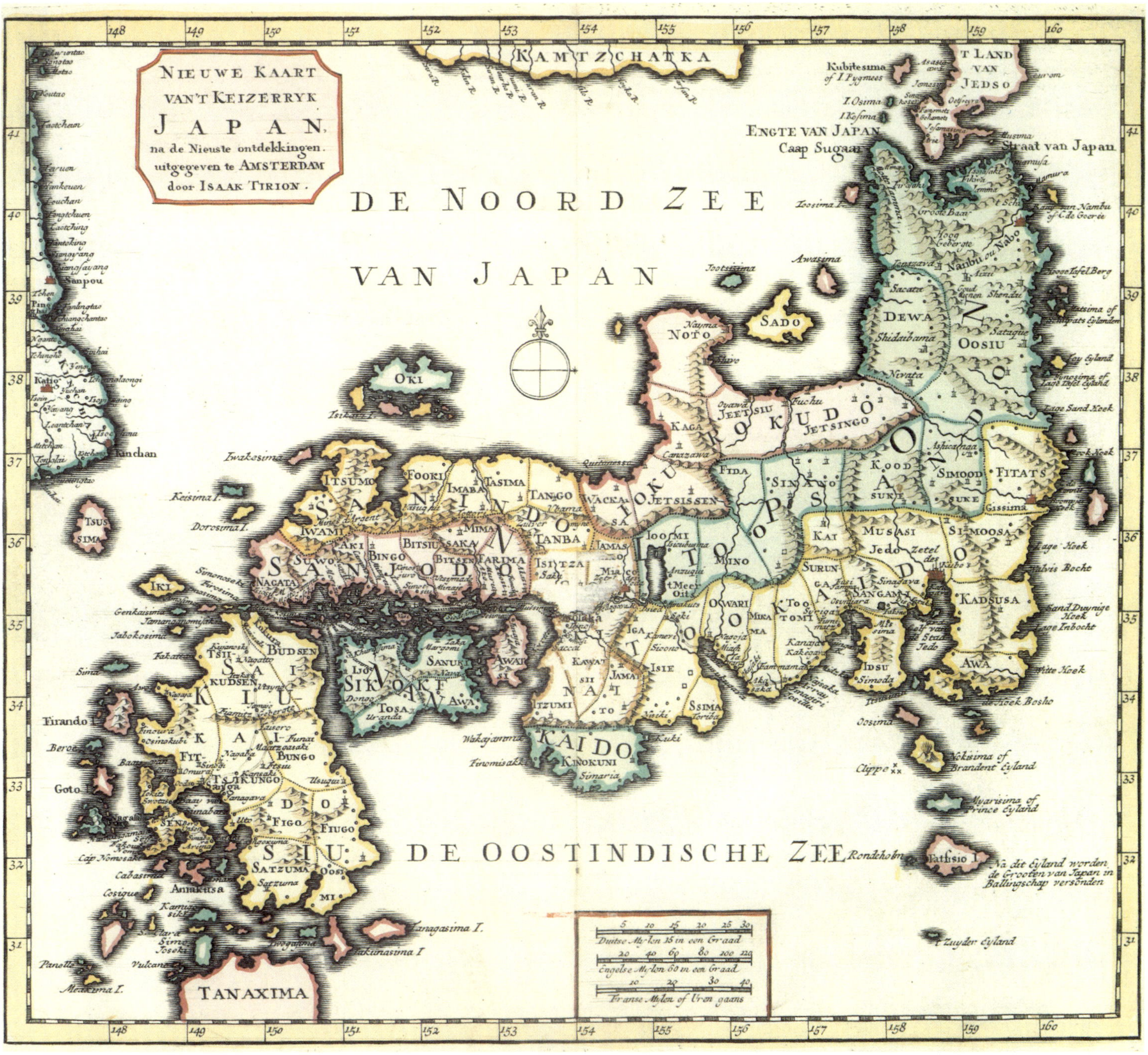

KAMTZCHATKA

DE NOORD ZEE

VAN JAPAN

'T LAND VAN JEDSO

ENGTE VAN JAPAN
Caap Sugaar

Straat van Japan

DEWA

OOSIU

OKI

NOTO
Sado
Awasima

ROKUDO

JETSINGO

ITSUMO
FOORI
IMABA
TASIMA
TANGO
WACKA
IOKU

SANINDO

IWAMI
AKI
BITSIU
SAKA
MIMA
TANBA

SANJODO

NAGATA

BUDSEN
SANUKI
AWA

SAI
KUDSEN
SIVOAKF
AWA
NAI

KILU-
KA

FIT-
TSIKUNGO

DO

FIGO
FIUGO

SIU

SATZUMA

KAIDO
KINOKUNI

DE OOSTINDISCHE ZEE

TANAXIMA

80. Isaac Tirion: *Nieuwe Kaart van't Keizerryk Japan*. Atlas leaf, ca. 1735, Amsterdam, 27.5×31.5 cm, author's collection.

A New and Accurate Map
of the
EMPIRE of JAPAN
Laid down
from the Memoirs of the
Portuguese and Dutch;
and particularly from the
Jesuit Missionaries,
as publish'd
by the Sr Bellin at Paris,
Being adjusted by
Astronomical Observations
By Eman. Bowen

Miles or Leagues of Japan
English Miles

THE SEA OF KOREA

THE SEA OF JAPAN

ORIENTAL OCEAN

The Country of KAMTSCHATKA

Streights of Kamtschatka

Cape Eurden

SADO I.

GULF OF SADO
Port of Niegata

NOTO

Cape Noto

OKI I.

TSUSSIMA

IKI I.

FIRANDO I.

Gotto I.

Meaxima I.

ISLE OF XIMO

DIEMEN STREIGHTS

ISLANDS OF LIQUEIO

ISLE OF XICOCO
OR I. OF HIU

FATSISIO I. where the
great Men are (by the Emperor)
sent into Exile

S.t Anthony
S.t Roch I.

THE Islands of Liqueio

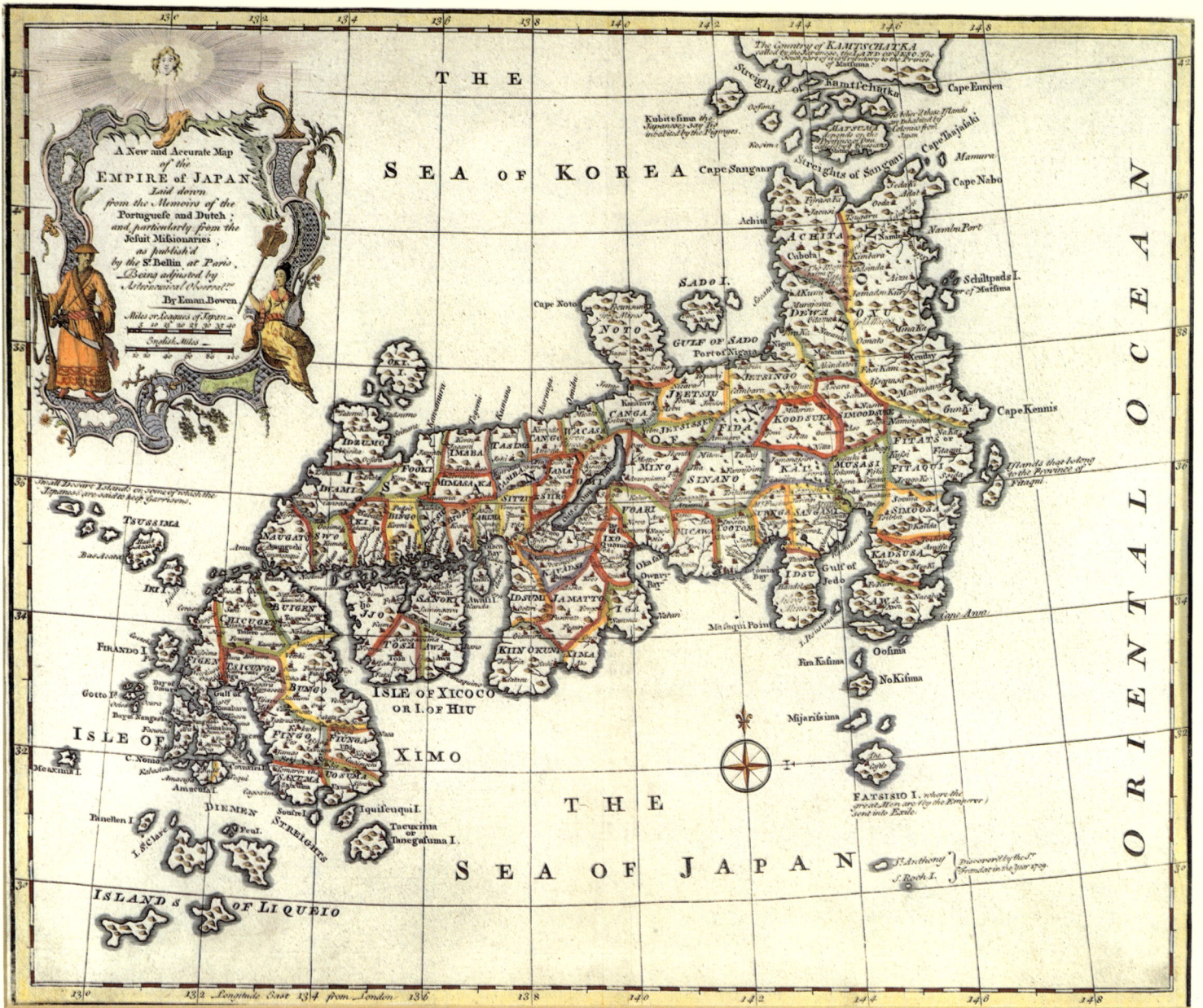

81. Emanuel Bowen: *A New and Accurate Map of the Empire of Japan*. Atlas leaf, 1747, London, 35.5 × 43 cm, author's collection. The way in which the area to the north of Honshu is depicted is noteworthy, as is the inclusion of the Land of Dwarves, seen in so many Japanese maps of the period.

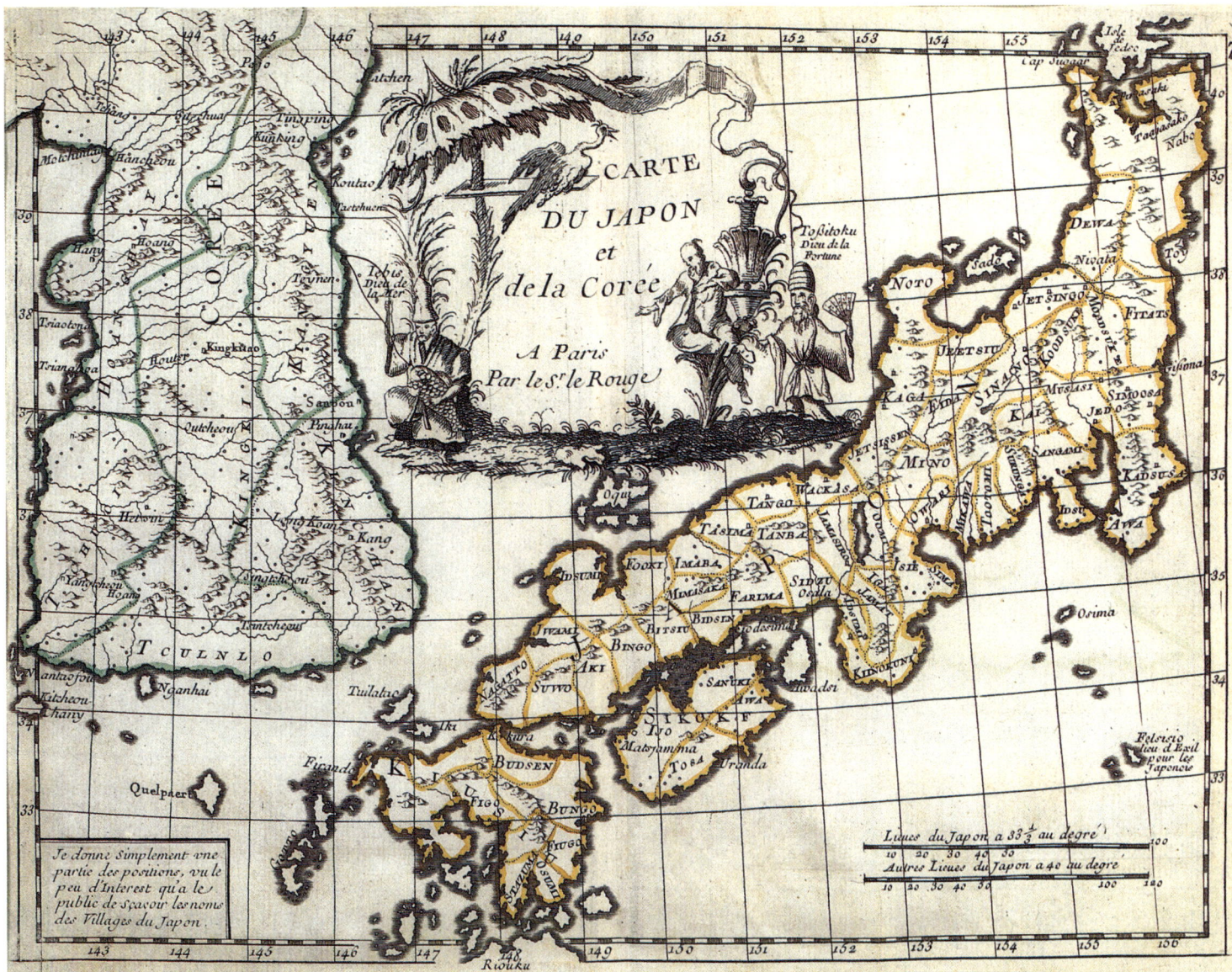

82 George Louis Lerouge: *Carte du Japon et de la Coreé*. Atlas leaf, 1748, Paris, 20 × 27.4 cm, author's collection. The cartouche recalls that of Kaempfer's map in Plate 76.

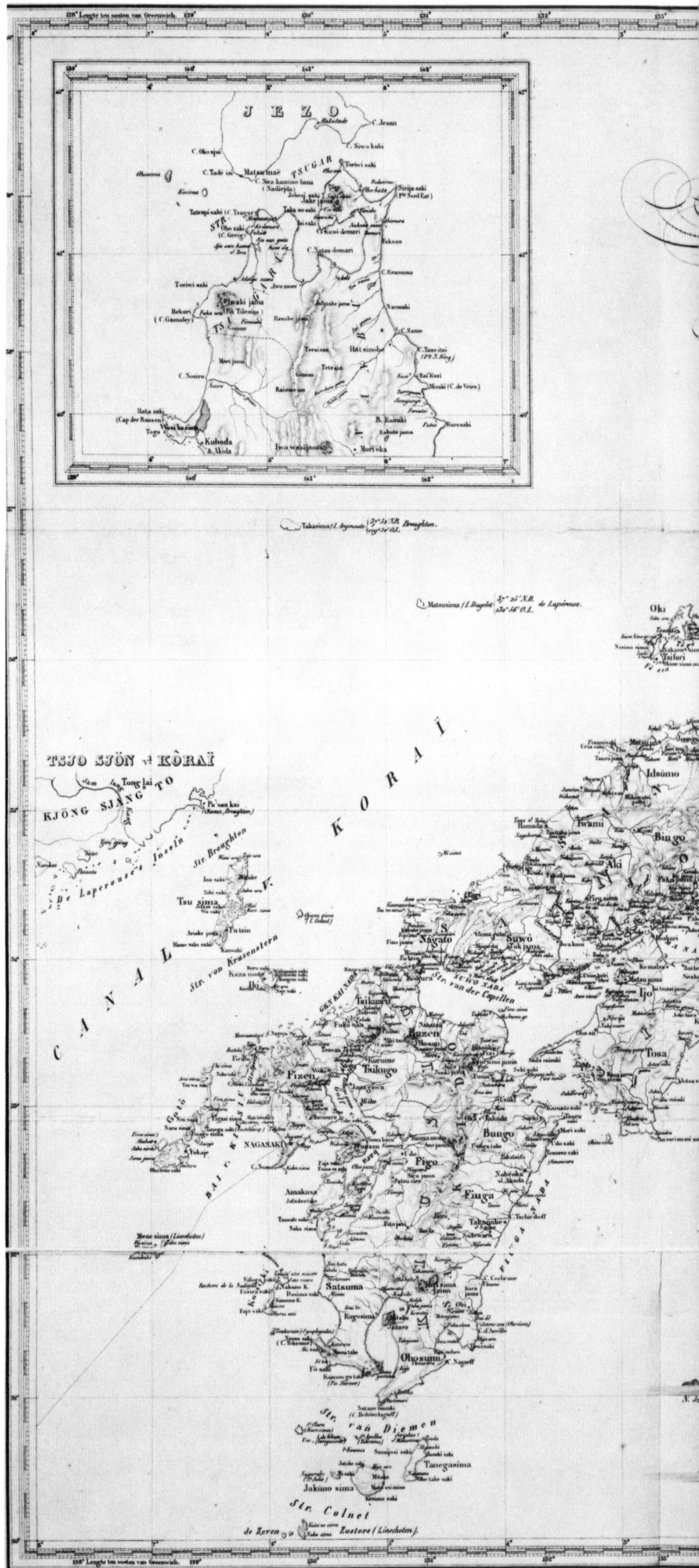

83. Philipp Franz von Siebold: *Japanisches Reich*. Atlas leaf, 1840, 39.5×55 cm, British Library, London.

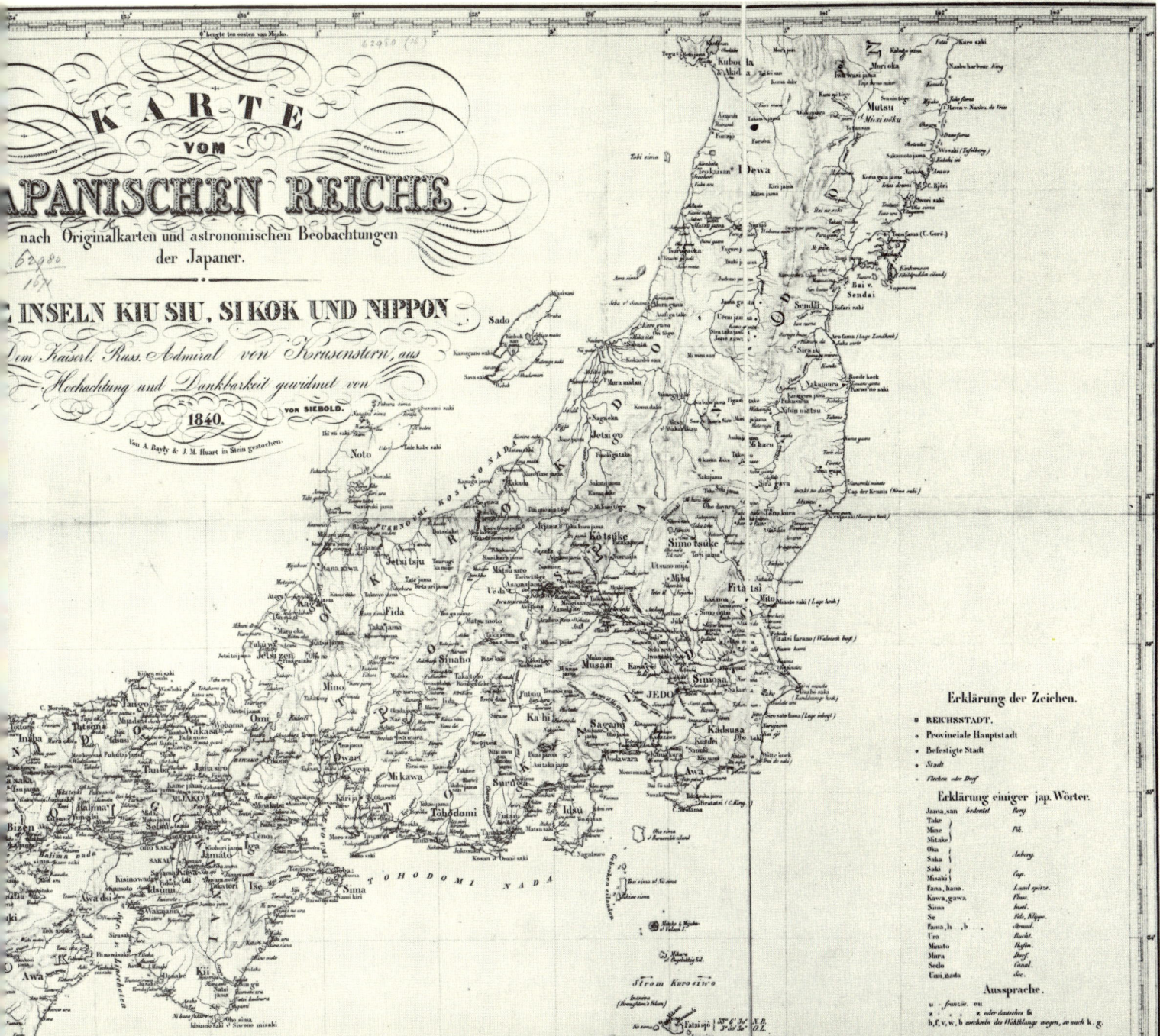

KARTE VOM JAPANISCHEN REICHE

nach Originalkarten und astronomischen Beobachtungen
der Japaner.

INSELN KIU SIU, SI KOK UND NIPPON

Dem Kaiserl. Russ. Admiral von Krusenstern, aus
Hochachtung und Dankbarkeit gewidmet von

1840. VON SIEBOLD.

Von A. Bayly & J. M. Huart in Stein gravochen.

Erklärung der Zeichen.

- REICHSSTADT.
- Provinciale Hauptstadt
- Befestigte Stadt
- Stadt
- Flecken oder Dorf

Erklärung einiger jap. Wörter.

Jama, yan	bedeutet	Berg.
Take		
Mine		Pik.
Mitake		
Oka		Anberg.
Saka		
Saki		Cap.
Misaki		
Fana, hama.		Land spitze.
Kawa, gawa		Fluss.
Sima		Insel.
Se		Fels, Klippe.
Fama, h... b...		Strand.
Ura		Bucht.
Masato		Hafen.
Mura		Dorf.
Sedo		Canal.
Umi, nada		See.

Aussprache.

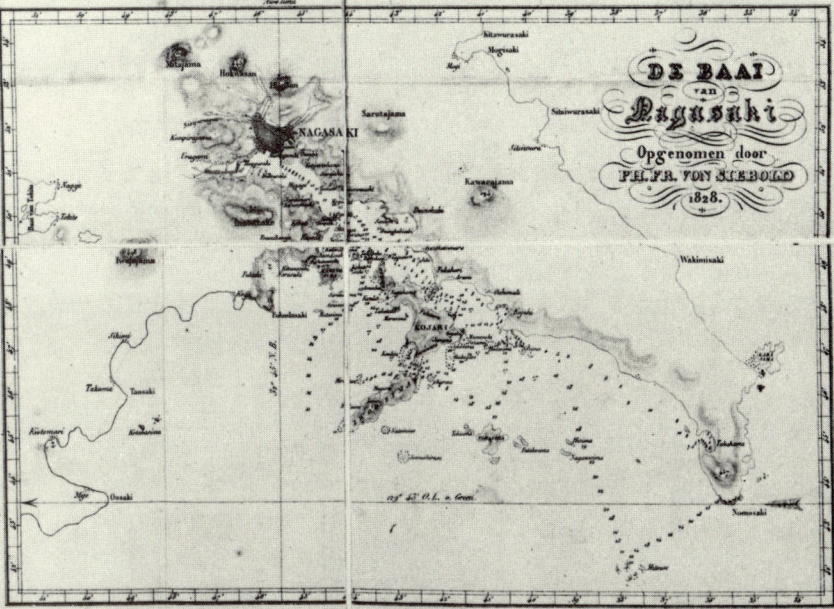

DE BAAI van **Nagasaki**
Opgenomen door
PH. FR. VON SIEBOLD
1828.

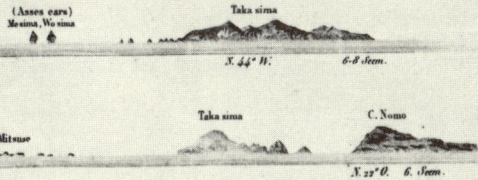

I. Meac sima. (Linschoten.)

(Asses ears)
Me sima, Wo sima

Taka sima
N. 44° W.   6-8 Seem.

Taka sima
Mitsue
N. 22° O.   6. Seem.

84. Girolamo de Angelis: map of Japan and Hokkaido. Manuscript, ca. 1621, 39.5×55 cm, Archivum Historicum, Society of Jesus, Rome.

JAPONÆ
ac
TERRÆ IESSONIS
Novissima Descriptio
Robt. Morden

Land of Jeſſo

Straite of Vries
Staten Iland
Canale of Piecko

Mataimay

Aquita

Sando I.

Nabo

E

Deua

Giſſima

COREA I.

Oqui I.

B

Tango

Vacata 7000

Jedo

jacama

Tau

C

Kamagawa

D

I. d'Ladrones al Quelpaerts

Fogui
Nagata
Simonisiki
Amangashi
Camenosacci
Meuwri
Binga

A

Abos
Iringane
Sanonsacci
Saciд Medvo

Dronge

Owarri
Mia
Occeſsacci

Naranya

Tonda

Tonda

Oduro

Toguxima

Kokero

Saccai

Falcone

Coſinda

Oatro

Owarri

Canmianumi

Falcone

Coſinda

Ongeluckigh I.

I. Firando

Oun war
Fiſen
Nan gaſacqui
Cam goxuma

Zuyder I.

Gotto I.

Arima

TONSAI.

Cikoko

Meacexima

BUNGO I.

Straite of Deimen

Tanaixima

A	Tamaystero
B	Ietſengo
C	Ietſeſen
D	Quanto
E	Ochio
F	Swoja
G	Dubo

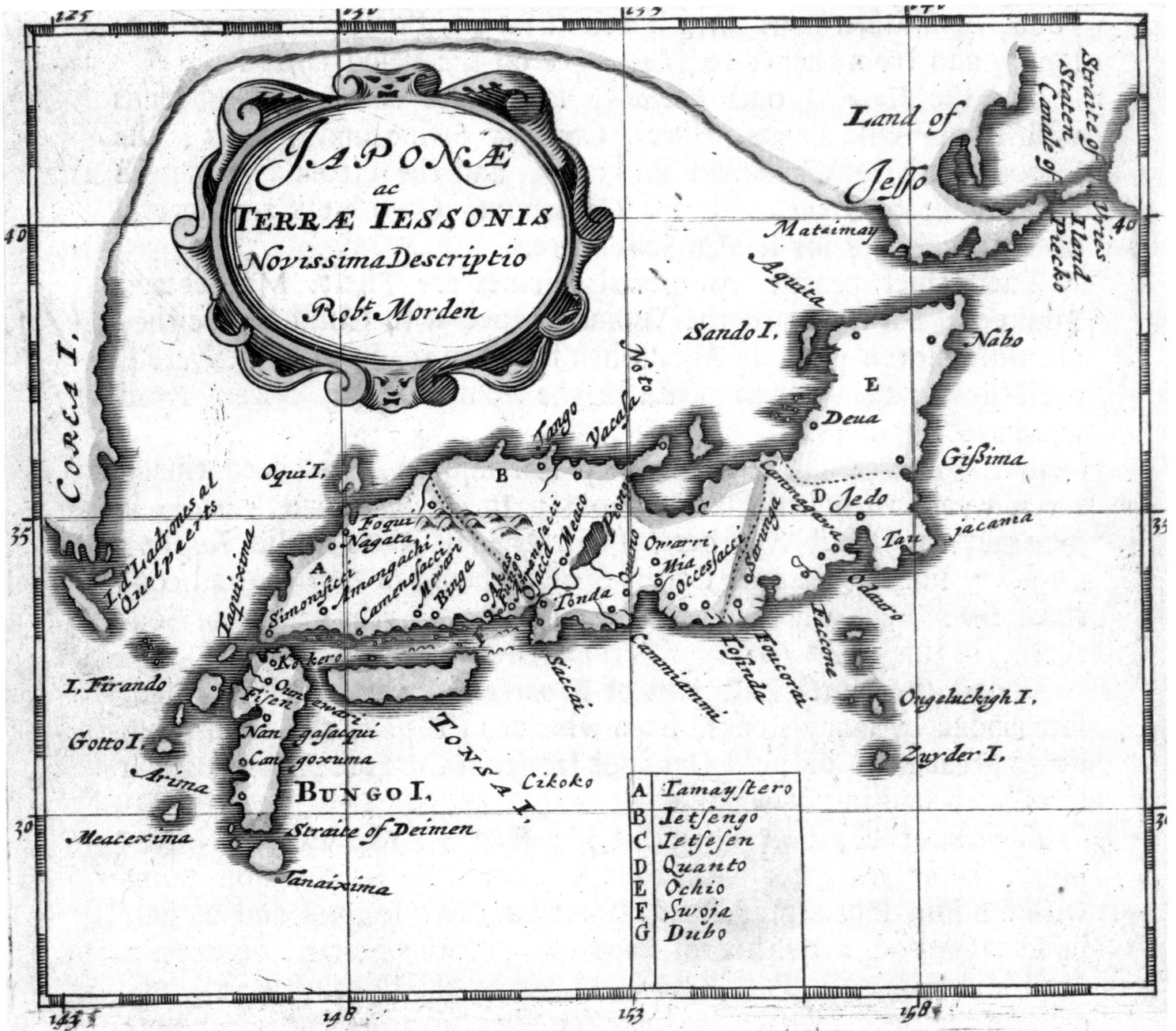

85. Robert Morden: *Japonae ac Terrae Iessonis Novissima Descriptio.* Atlas leaf, 1680, London, 10.5 × 12.5 cm, author's collection. Morden's map is interesting for the way in which Hokkaido (Jesso) is shown as being connected to Korea (Corea).

86. Guillaume Delisle: *L'Asie*. Early eighteenth century, 46×58 cm, author's collection.

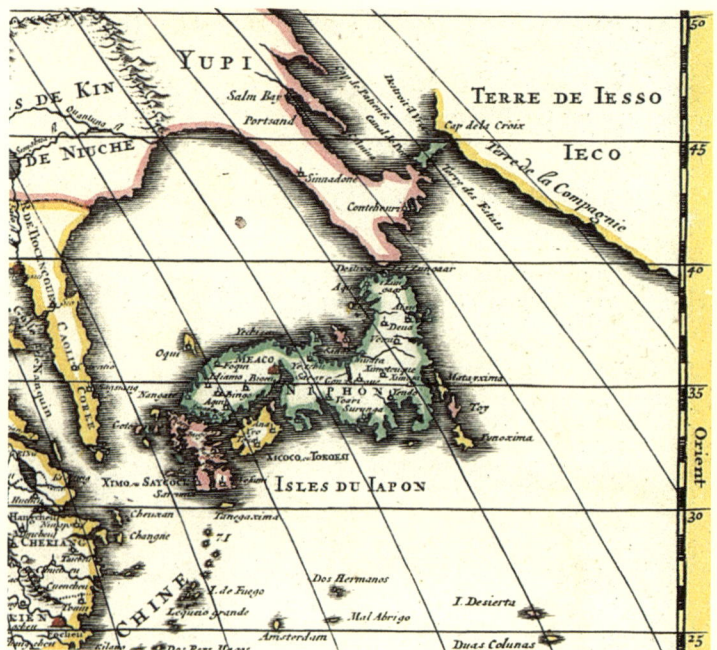

87. Detail, 11.4×13.5 cm, from Plate 86. The confusion concerning the northern territories is quite evident in this depiction of the region. A comparison with the maps of Jansson (Pl. 70) and Coronelli (Pl. 75) reveals the shifting locales and proportions of Yupi (Manchuria?), Compagniesland (Etorofu), and Ezo, which looms large in the northeast.

160

88. *A New Map of Grand Tartary and China.* Early eighteenth century, 35.5 × 50 cm, author's collection. This map is dedicated to His Highness Willliam Duke of Gloucester and is said to be taken from "Mr. de Fer's Map of Asia." This presumably refers to the French cartographer, Nicholas de Fer (1646–1720).

89. Detail, 12.3 × 13.9 cm, from Plate 88. Though the coast of Manchuria extends much too far eastward, "Jeso" is correctly depicted as an island.

90. J. and F. Tallis: *Japan and Corea*. Atlas leaf, 1851, London and New York, 26×34 cm, author's collection. The scene inset at top center is reproduced from the Montanus illustration of Edo (Pl. 72), and the ship at lower right is very similar to those in Plate 75.

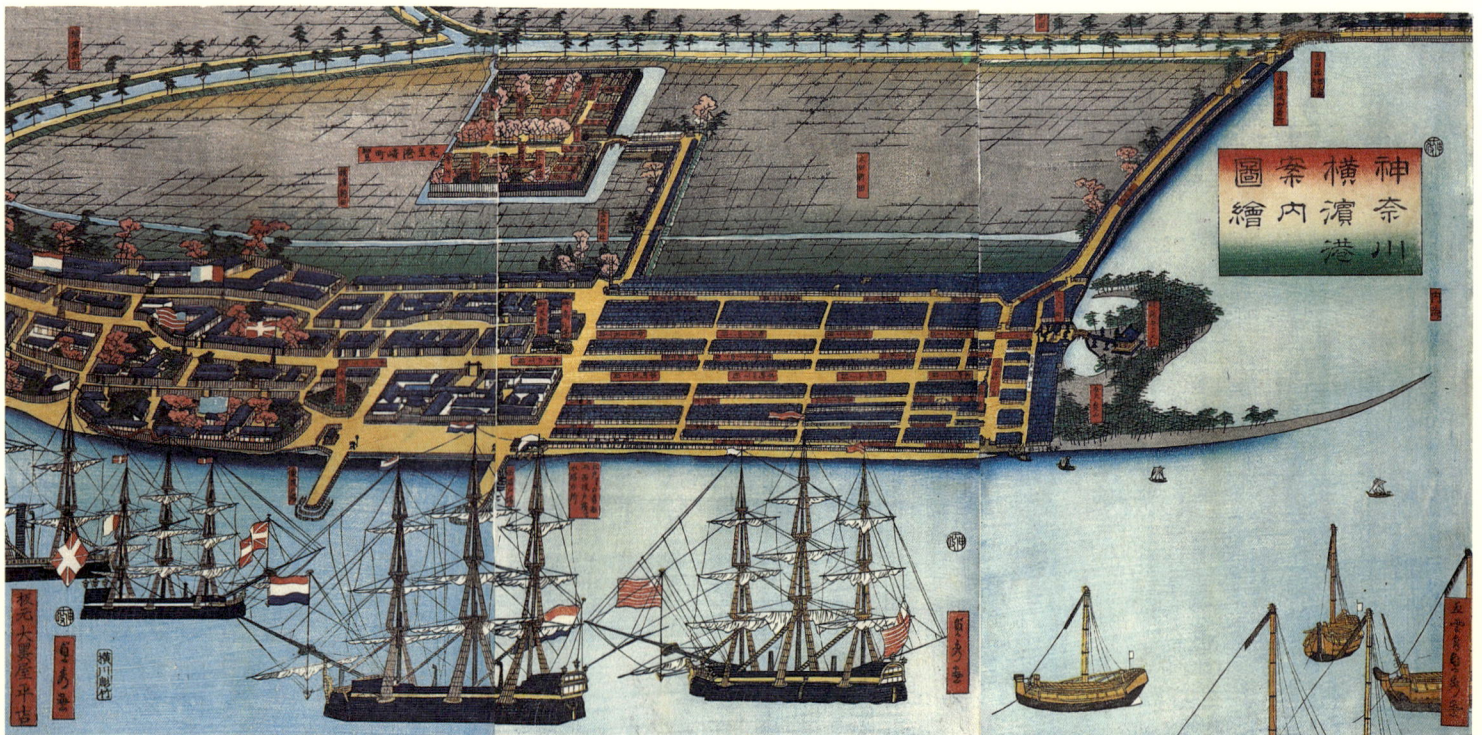

91. Sadahide: *Kanagawa Yokohama-kō Annai Zu-e* (Map-guide to Yokohama Port, Kanagawa). Woodblock print, dated 1860, 36×76 cm, Maspro Denkow Art Gallery, Nagoya. The British, American, and French ships in the foreground are a sign of the times, as Japan opened her doors to the West in the mid-nineteenth century.

Annotated Bibliography

WORKS IN ENGLISH

Aihara, Ryōichi. "Ignacio Moreira's Geographical Activities in Japan (1590–92)." *Tōyō Bunko* No. 34 (1976): 209–42.

*

Alcock, Rutherford. *The Capital of the Tycoon*. London, 1863.

An account by the first British Minister to Japan, 1859–62. Fascinating if you skip some of the more long-winded passages.

*

Aston, W.G., tr. *Nihongi*. Reprinted. Tokyo, 1980.

The *Nihongi* is one of the two oldest Japanese chronicles. Aston was a British scholar-diplomat of the late nineteenth century.

*

Ayusawa, Shintaro. "The Types of World Maps Made in Japan's Age of National Isolation." *Imago Mundi* 10 (1967): 123–28.

*

Beans, George H. *A List of Japanese Maps of the Tokugawa Era*. Jenkintown, 1951. Supplements A, B, and C, 1955–63.

Invaluable to anyone trying to identify and date an early printed Japanese map.

*

Boxer, Charles. *The Christian Century in Japan*. California and London, 1951.

———. *Jan Compagnie in Japan*. The Hague, 1950.

———. *The Great Ship from Amacon*. Lisbon, 1960.

Professor Boxer is one of the undoubted experts on the Dutch and Portuguese connection with Japan. His study of Japan's Christian century is very readable as well as informative.

*

Campbell, Tony. *Early Maps*. London, 1981.

———. *Japan: European Printed Maps to 1800*. Map Collector's Series 4, No. 36. London, 1967.

The first book, beautifully produced with many color illustrations, is an excellent introduction for anyone beginning to be interested in old maps. The second is essential for anyone collecting old European maps of Japan. Many black-and-white illustrations and details of various maps are listed.

*

Caron, François, and Joost Schouten. *A True Description of the Mighty Kingdoms of Japan and Siam*. Reprinted from the English edition of 1663, with an introduction by C.R. Boxer. London, 1935.

An account which is primarily of interest because it shows what an intelligent foreign observer was able to learn and thought worth recording in the seventeenth century.

*

Catalogue of an Exhibition of Chinese and Japanese Maps. British Museum, London, 1974.

An interesting collection of Japanese maps made by one of the world's great scholarly institutions.

*

Collis, Maurice. *The Grand Peregrination Being the Life and Adventures of Fernão Mendes Pinto*. London, 1949.

Interesting, even if partly fictional.

*

Cooper Michael, ed. *They Came to Japan: An Anthology of European Reports on Japan, 1534–1640*. California and London, 1965, 1982.

———, ed. *The Southern Barbarians: The First Europeans in Japan*. Tokyo, 1971.

———. *Rodrigues the Interpreter*. Tokyo, 1974.

———. *This Island of Japon: João Rodrigues' Account of 16th-Century Japan*. Tokyo and New York, 1973.

———. "Rodrigues in China: The Letters of João Rodrigues 1611–1633," in *Kokugo-shi e no Michi*, ed. Doi Sensei Shōju Kinen Rombun-shū Kankōkai, 353–224. Tokyo, 1981.

Dr. Michael Cooper, the editor of *Monumenta Nipponica,* has made a special study of João Rodrigues as well as of the European contacts with Japan in the sixteenth and seventeenth centuries. All his books are scholarly, informative and absorbing.

*

Cortazzi, Sir Hugh. "Old Maps of Japan." *Transactions of the Asiatic Society of Japan.* 3rd ser. 17 (1982): 53–119.

*

Gardner, K.B. "Englebert Kaempfer's Japanese Library." *Asia Major* 7 (1959).

Explains how Kaempfer's books and maps came into the possession of what is now the British Library.

*

Goedertier, Joseph M. *A Dictionary of Japanese History*. Tokyo and New York, 1968.

A useful general reference work.

*

Goss, J.E.S. "Map of Japan by Urbano Monti." *The Map Collector,* No. 15 (1981): 18–22.

*

Harrison, John A. "Notes on the Discovery of Ezo." *Annals of the Association of American Geographers* 50, No. 3 (September 1958): 254–66.

*

Hoyanagi, Mutsumi. "Reappreciation of Inō's Maps, the First Maps of Japan Based on Actual Survey." *Geographical Reports of Tokyo Metropolitan University* 2 (1967): 147–62.

*

Ihara, Saikaku. *The Life of an Amorous Man (Kōshoku Ichidai Otoko),* translated by Kenji Hamada. Tokyo, 1963.

*

Kaempfer Engelbert. *The History of Japan.* London, 1727.

The conscientious and careful efforts which Kaempfer made to study and record what he could of Japan during his time in the country from 1690 to 1692 make this one of the most fascinating of old books on Japan.

*

Keene, Donald. *The Japanese Discovery of Europe.* London, 1952.

A useful survey of Japanese efforts to study Western learning during the years of seclusion. Professor Keene is one of the outstanding American scholars of Japan and the Japanese.

*

Kerr, George H. *Okinawa–The History of an Island People.* Tokyo, 1958.

*

Kish [Kiss], George. "Some Aspects of the Missionary Cartographers of Japan during the 16th century." *Imago Mundi* 7 (1949): 39–41.

————. "The Japan in the Mural Atlas of the Palazzo Vecchio Florence." *Imago Mundi* 8 (1951): 52–54.

————. "The Cartography of Japan during the middle Tokugawa Period: A study in cross-cultural influences." *Annals of the Association of American Geographers* 37, No. 2 (June 1967): 101–19.

George Kish (or Kiss) has made a considerable contribution to the study of old maps of Japan.

*

Kitagawa, Kay. "The Map of Hokkaido of G. de Angelis, ca. 1621." *Imago Mundi* 7 (1950): 110–14.

*

Knobel, E.B. "Ino Chukei and the First Surveys of Japan." *Geographical Journal* 62 (1913): 246–50.

*

Kubo, Chōhei. "A summary of my studies of Girolamo de Angelis' Yezo Map." *Imago Mundi* 10 (1953): 81–86.

*

Lach, Donald F. *Asia in the Making of Europe.* Vol. 1, *The Century of Discovery.* Chicago, 1965.

An interesting and comprehensive survey.

*

Lister, Raymond. *Old Maps and Globes.* London, 1965.

Useful background on mapmaking and mapmakers with comments on globes, decorations on maps, and watermarks.

*

Mills, D.D. *A Collection of Tales from Uji: A Study and Translation of Uji Shūi Monogatari.* Cambridge, 1970.

*

Mody, N.H.N. *A Collection of Nagasaki Colour Prints and Paintings.* Tokyo, 1969.

165

Only of marginal interest in connection with the present work, but a well-produced and fascinating book.

*

Nakamura, Hiroshi. *East Asia in Old Maps.* Honolulu, 1963.

―――. "The Japanese Portolanos of Portuguese Origin of the XVIth and XVIIth centuries." *Imago Mundi* 18 (1964): 24–44.

―――. "Old Japanese World Maps Preserved by the Koreans." *Imago Mundi* 4 (1947): 3–22.

Professor Nakamura's works provide very useful information.

*

O'Donoghue, Yolande. "Map Makers of Old Japan." *Geographical Magazine* 47, No. 1, (October 1974): 40–47.

*

Ogilby, John. *Atlas Japannensis. Collected out of their several writings and journals by Montanus Arnoldus.* London, 1670.

This account is as much of interest for its imaginary as for its realistic elements.

*

Ōtani, Ryōkichi. *Tadataka Inō, the Japanese Land Surveyor.* Translated by Sugimura Kazue. Tokyo, 1932.

*

Polo, Marco. *Travels.* Translated by Ronald Latham. London, 1958.

The first Western account of Japan.

*

Pye, N., and W.G. Beaseley. "An Unde-

scribed Manuscript Copy of Inō Chūkei's Map of Japan." *Geographical Journal* 117, (1950): 178–87.

*

Ramming, M. "The Evolution of Cartography in Japan. *Imago Mundi* 2 (1937): 17–21.

*

Ramsay, R.H. *No Longer on the Map.* New York, 1972.

The Straits of Anian were by no means the only geographical feature which old mapmakers invented, as this intriguing work demonstrates.

*

Sansom, G.B.A. *Japan: A Short Cultural History.* Revised edition. London, 1946.

―――. *A History of Japan.* 3 volumes. London, 1958, 1961, 1964.

―――. *The Western World and Japan.* London, 1950.

Sir George Sansom's books provide probably the best introduction for the English reader to the history and culture of Japan.

*

Saris, John. *The Voyage of John Saris to Japan, 1613.* Hakluyt Society, London, 1900, 1967.

Read in conjunction with the diaries of Richard Cocks, it gives a firsthand account of William Adams and the English factory at Hirado in the early seventeenth century.

*

Schütte, J.F. "Map of Japan by Father Girolamo de Angelis." *Imago Mundi* 9 (1952): 73–78.

―――. "Ignacio Moreira of Lisbon: Cartographer in Japan, 1590–1592." *Imago Mundi* 16 (1962): 116–28.

————. "Japanese Cartography at the Court of Florence: Robert Dudley's Maps of Japan, 1606–1636." *Imago Mundi* 23 (1969): 29–58.

Father Schütte's scholarly articles provide much interesting information.

*

Skelton, R.A. *Explorers' Maps*. London, 1958.

————. *History of Cartography*. London, 1963.

Both these books provide useful background and are well illustrated. *Explorers' Maps* concentrates on the history of maps arising from exploration. The *History of Cartography* is both more general and comprehensive. The section on Japan is brief.

*

Thames, Richard. *Servant of the Shōgun*. Tenterden, England, 1981.

A readable account of the life of William Adams.

*

Tooley, R.V. *Dictionary of Map Makers*. Tring, 1979.

A very useful work of reference.

*

Tsukahira, Toshio G. *Feudal Control in Tokugawa Japan: The Sankin Kōtai System*. Harvard East Monographs No. 20, 1966.

*

Ury, Marian, tr. *Tales of Times Now Past: Sixty-two Stories from a Medieval Japanese Collection*. California and London, 1979.

A translation of the *Konjaku Monogatari*, one source of tales concerning the Rakshas and Rasetsukoku.

*

Watanabe, Akira. *Cartography in Japan, Past and Present*. Tokyo, 1980.

JAPANESE WORKS

Akioka, Takejiro. *Nihonchizu-shi*. Tokyo, 1955.

This book provides a full and careful account of the development of mapmaking in Japan with some references to European mapmaking, but it is not comprehensive on the latter.

*

Cieslik, Hubert. *Hoppō Tankenki*. Tokyo, 1962. A study of the exploration of Hokkaido and the northern territories.

Hirooka, Tomoo. "Koji Garan Chujikusenhōi to Kōkochijiki." *Kōkogaku Zasshi*. 62, No. 1 (1976): 49–63.

*

Matsumoto, Ken'ichi, ed. *Namban Kōmō Nihonchizu Shūsei*. Tokyo, 1975.

A major study of Western maps of Japan in the sixteenth and seventeenth centuries. Numerous illustrations in full color.

Namba, Matsutarō, et al. *Nihon no Kochizu.* Tokyo, 1969.

A useful and well-illustrated survey of old Japanese maps of Japan by the best Japanese scholars of this subject. Namba's collection has been presented to the Kobe City Museum.

*

Oda, Takeo. *Chizu no Rekishi.* Tokyo, 1973.

————. *Kochizu no Sekai.* Tokyo, 1980.

Both of these are informative and scholarly.

*

Okamoto, Yoshitomo. *Jūrokuseiki Sekaichizujō no Nihon.* Tokyo, 1938.

*

Ono, Tadashige. *Nihon Furuezu Shūsei.* Tokyo, 1974.

A study mainly of local Japanese maps, profusely illustrated.

*

Umeki Tsūtoku. *Ezo Kochizu Monogatari.* Sapporo, 1974.

*

Unno, K., et al. *Nihon Kochizu Taisei.* 2 Vols. *Nihonzuhen* and *Sekaizuhen.* Tokyo, 1974.

These two magnificently produced and illustrated volumes are the most comprehensive books available on old maps of Japan.

*

Yamori, Kazuhiko. *Toshizu no rekishi, Nihonhen.* Tokyo, 1974.

A comprehensive survey of Japanese city and town maps.

WORKS IN OTHER EUROPEAN LANGUAGES

Boscaro, Adriana. *Ezo (oggi Hokkaido) nella Storia della Cartografia Europea,* Sec. 17–18. Florence, 1981.

A useful and detailed survey.

*

Cortesão, Armando, and A. Teixeira da Mota. *Portugaliae Monumenta Cartographica.* 6 Vols. Lisbon, 1960.

This is indeed a monumental work, and the section on Japan in English (Vol. 5, pp. 170–78) provides a valuable analysis of sixteenth- and seventeenth-century maps of Japan.

Dahlgren, E.W. *Les Débuts de la Cartographie du Japon.* Upsala, 1911.

A careful analysis of sixteenth-century maps depicting Japan.

*

Nachod, O. *Zur Kartographie Japans: Zeitschrift der Gesellschaft fur Erdkunde Zu.* Berlin, 1910.

*

Nakamura Hiroshi. *Les Cartes du Japon que servient de models aux cartographes Europeens . . . .* Tokyo, 1966–67.

Nakamura's studies have made a significant contribution to knowledge of Japanese maps.

168

Siebold, Ph. Fr. von. *Nippon Archiv zur Be-schreibung von Japan: Eine biographische Skizze.* 2nd ed. Würzburg and Leipzig, 1897.

*

Teleki, Paul Graf. *Atlas zur Geschichte der Karto-graphie der Japanischen Inseln.* Budapest, 1909.

This weighty tome (metaphorically and literally) remains a major source of information about Western maps of Japan. Copiously illustrated, it is a scholarly work of major importance in this field.

Index

172

174

The "weathermark" identifies this book as a production of John Weather-hill, Inc., publishers of fine books on Asia and the Pacific. Supervising editor: Jeffrey Hunter. Book design and typography: Miriam F. Yamaguchi. Layout of illustrations: Yutaka Shimoji. Production supervisor: Mitsuo Okado. Composition of text: Samhwa Printing Company, Seoul. Printing: Kenkyusha Printing Company, Tokyo. Engraving and printing of the plates, in four-color and monochrome offset: Nissha Printing Company, Kyoto. Binding: Okamoto Binderies, Tokyo. The typeface used is Monotype Perpetua.